The Ramayana

Smt. Chitra Ramaswamy

Prism Books Pvt Ltd
Bengaluru • chennai • Hyderabad • Kochi

The Ramayana

Smt. Chitra Ramaswamy

Published by:

Prism Books Pvt. Ltd.

1865, 32nd Cross, 10th Main
BSK II Stage, Bengaluru - 560 070.
Phone: 080-26714108 | Telefax: 080-26713979
email: logistics@prismbooks.com
www.prismbooks.com

Also at:

Chennai	:	044-24311244, prismchennai@prismbooks.com
Hyderabad	:	040-27612938, prismhyderabad@prismbooks.com
Kochi	:	0484-4000945, prismkochi@prismbooks.com
Kolkata	:	09831537010, prismkolkata@prismbooks.com

Layout design	:	Prism Books Pvt. Ltd.,
Cover Design	:	Chandranath Acharya
ISBN	:	978-93-86506-14-6
Price	:	₹ 175
Total Pages	:	172
Printed at	:	Adithya Printers, Bengaluru.

Dedicated to the memory of my grandparents

Ranganayaki & P. R. Krishnamurthy Iyengar

&

Sulochana & Dr. K. S. Rangaswamy Iyengar

Acknowledgement

In all humility I offer my heartfelt gratitude to the Almighty for opening this window of opportunity to enable me to embark on a spiritual journey in re-narrating this monumental story of the Lord.

I offer my sincere thanks to Shri. Pranesh S, Managing Director, of Prism Books Pvt. Ltd., and Shri Subba Rao, former CEO of Amrita Bharati, Bharatiya Vidya Bhavan, for reposing faith in me and asking me to retell this Divine epic, a most daunting task. This work would not have been possible but for the constant encouragement the two of them gave me through its progress. I was especially inspired and motivated by Mr. Subba Rao's guidance and suggestions at various stages which also allowed me perceptions that enabled me to recount a saga of such mammoth proportions, without bias.

I acknowledge in all humbleness the several erudite and scholarly personalities who have narrated the Ramayana through the ages, and whose books I have been reading since childhood. The starting point among them was the all-time favourite *Ramayana* by Sri C. Rajagopalachari. I refreshed my memory with various versions of the epic including Srimad Valmiki Ramayana by Gita Press, Ramcharitramanas of Sri Tulsidas, Kamba Ramayana and contemporary writings on it.

My research on the *Ramayana* before embarking on this monumental work also led me to listen to discourses in Tamil by scholars on the subject.

My parents, husband, son and daughter, contributed to my endeavour by recalling episodes from the epic to help me keep my narrative close to the classic version as revealed by the great sage, Valmiki. I do not have enough words to thank my sister, Mrs. Sowmya Rangarajan, whose contribution towards editing this work, has been monumental.

Finally, for every one of my books published by Prism Books Pvt. Ltd., I would remain thankful to Mr. Sreesha Belakvadi and Mrs. Nalini Murali for introducing me to the publishers.

Chitra Ramaswamy.

The Ramayana

My first exposure to the epics, and Ramayana in particular, came about when I was still in my single digit years. It was through my paternal grandmother who stayed with us. She was a good story teller, who would carry stories through to their conclusion with expressive eyes and a voice that articulated so well, the emotion experienced by each character.

I wonder at the number of times she'd have regaled me with episodes from the Ramayana, Mahabharata, Krishna Leela and a string of other tales from mythology — Dhruva, Prahlad, Satyavan-Savithri — the list could go on.

Well, those were years when I saw everything - people and characters only in two colours - black and white. There were no shades of grey. Kaikeyi, Ravana, Manthara, Soorpanakha and a host of others snugly fit into the black slot. The amusing and adorable Hanuman who sported a ridiculously long tail and had a capacity to assume any size, who thought and acted like a human being, was obviously white. The protagonist, Rama, his consort, brothers and many others who helped them during their years of exile, were all the good people labelled white.

Ramayana to me, then, was just another fairy tale except that Rama and Hanuman were gods who we worshipped, and prayed to. However, years later, as I sat down to pen this prose of mammoth proportions, the task before me appeared overwhelming. Questions that I had not raised as a kid, reared their head through adolescence and led me on a quest, seeking answers. Several reads of Valmiki's version and other interpretations of the *Ramayana* only added to my confusion. Paradoxes and contradictions were many when I viewed the epic from a plethora of angles – the moral, ethical, logical, practical, and the mythological.

It was indeed a paradox that I myself experienced – retelling the *Ramayana* was at once easy, and tough, when Mr. Subba Rao asked me to keep the storyline in line with Valmiki's classic version! I present this narrative in the hope I have done justice to the classic poem.

Chitra Ramaswamy

Contents

Princes of Ayodhya

The kingdom of Kosala, stretched along the banks of the Sarayu River. Nourished by the waters of the Sarayu, the land was rich with fruit orchards and emerald green plants hosting a myriad of brightly colored flowers. Its granaries were brimming with abundant grains and its coffers were ever full. The kingdom of plenty experienced no want. Its capital Ayodhya was fringed by the river on all sides except the south. The fortified city of exceptional splendor was designed by Vaivaswata Manu, ruler of the Solar Dynasty.

Dasharatha, the illustrious ruler of Kosala was a descendent of Ikshvaku, Manu's eldest son. He was well versed in the Vedas and was known for his sagacity and benevolence. The monarch was just as famed for his skills in administration as for his expertise in the art of warfare. He enhanced his administrative prowess with assistance from an able council of ministers who oversaw the safety and security of their king and kingdom.

Kosala prospered under Dasharatha and its people lived in joy, harmony and peace. A single factor marred the king's happiness. Dasharatha and his three wives, Kausalya, Sumitra and Kaikeyi were saddened by the absence of a progeny to carry on his lineage. In consultation with family, elders and learned sages, the king decided to perform a or fire sacrifice to beget offspring.

The sacrificial ground was identified and appropriately prepared on the northern bank of the Sarayu. The assembled sages, scholars and priests, under the direction of the great sage, Rishyashringa, chanted mantras and poured offerings into the sacred fire.

The devas who had congregated to participate in the yajna, made use of this opportunity to seek Lord Vishnu's help in dealing with Ravana, the lord of Lanka. The rakshasa king had terrorized them and made their lives miserable. Ravana who had once performed severe austerities to please Brahma, obtained a boon from him that made him invincible against all gods, celestial beings, yakshas and ogres. Emboldened by the boon, he struck terror in all the three worlds and harassed the devas.

The devas now turned to Vishnu and begged him to save them. Lord Vishnu responded to their pleas and vowed to be born on earth, as a human being. For, in his arrogance Ravana had sought no protection against ordinary mortals. And what better opportunity to fulfill his pledge than the one present now, when the illustrious Dasharatha was praying for a son!

The atmosphere reverberated with the powerful chanting of mantras, and resonated with the melody of musical instruments. Suddenly, a figure resplendent in all glory, arose from the sacrificial flame. The radiant form, held out a bowl of *payasam* and addressed Dasharatha: "Distribute this divine *payasam* that has been especially prepared by the god, to your wives. Rest assured that in due course you will be blessed with four strong, pious and powerful sons."

Dasharatha who was overjoyed on hearing this, bowed reverentially before the figure and circumambulated it. He handed over the *payasam* to his three wives.

Birth of the princes

The following spring, Ayodhya welcomed with jubilation, the birth of four princes of the Ikshvaku dynasty. Dasharatha beamed with pride and delight as he admired his four sons, Rama, whom Kausalya held close to her bosom, Bharata, the son born of his favourite queen Kaikeyi and the twins Lakshmana and Shatrugna nursed by their mother Sumitra. The king marked the auspicious event by making generous gifts of gold, jewels, cows and other forms of wealth to the dancers, musicians, bards and priests.

The princes grew up in an atmosphere of love and care. A special bond developed between Rama and Lakshmana as did deep affection and companionship between Bharata and Shatrugna. The youngsters were initiated to formal education under Vasishta at his hermitage. The princes delighted in the pastoral environs of the ashram. They thrilled at the kinks of green pasture, dotted with young lambs and deer, alongside the rivulets. They enjoyed the enchanting chirping of birds from their perch on fruit and flower laden trees. They took pleasure in the interesting and amiable interactions they had with other pupils in the Gurukula.

The brothers received training in various aspects of life as befitting imperials. They became proficient in the Vedas, mastered the art of using weapons and absorbed every form of learning under the shrewd guidance of Vasishta. Their learnings made them modest and humble and they endeared themselves to the citizens of Kosala.

Once their training was complete, Dasharatha contemplated the princes' wedding, in consultation with his family priests and other elders.

Vishwamitra

It was at that opportune moment that the great sage Vishwamitra arrived at Dasharatha's court. The king greeted him with due courtesy and expressed pleasure at having his esteemed presence in their midst. Vishwamitra who was pleased with the hospitality shown to him, immediately communicated to Dasharatha the reason for his visit. He asked Dasharatha to allow prince Rama accompany him to his hermitage to fight Maricha and Subahu, demons who threatened to destroy a yajna the rishi was performing.

Dasharatha became apprehensive of his young Rama facing danger from the demons. He was therefore reluctant to accede to Vishwamitra's request. However, he humbly said: "Why Rama, he is barely sixteen! How will he be able to combat the seasoned demons you mention? Oh learned seer, along with my extremely experienced and valiant army, I will myself guard your sacrifice and oversee its success by dealing with these ogres."

Vishwamitra was insistent on taking Rama with him. He further elaborated his cause to the king. "Mareecha and Subahu fight on behalf of the fearful demon Ravana, the son of sage Visrava and half-brother of Kubera. It is at his behest that these two rakshasas hinder my yajna."

Dasharatha was terrified at the very idea of exposing Rama to demons from Ravana's army. He was firm in his resolve to protect his dear son. He appealed to Vishwamitra saying, "When I myself have been unable to fend off the vile and violent Ravana, how will my tender

Rama, who I begot after so much *tapas*, confront his lot! I will accompany my army and encounter the demons sent by Ravana. Please spare my child Rama!"

The seer who radiated effulgence was known and feared for his fiery temper. Anger welled up in him as he heard Dasharatha. The ever wise Vasishta quickly intercepted and diffused the situation. He advised Dasharatha to send Rama with Vishwamitra by extolling the virtues, skills and superior learning of the rishi. "There is none on earth who is more knowledgeable in the use of various missiles as Vishwamitra. He is an epitome of dharma and is endowed with the power to see the past and divine the future. Though capable of dealing with the ogres himself, it is for Rama's good that he implores you to send him. This will be a good learning experience for the prince. Being protected by Vishwamitra, Rama will come to no harm from the demons."

Dasharatha felt reassured by Vasishta's words. He consented to send Rama with Vishwamitra. Rama's constant companion and shadow Lakshmana, joined his brother on the mission. Flowers rained from the heavens upon Dasharatha's sons as they walked step for step alongside Vishwamitra with bows and a quiver full of arrows slung over their shoulders. Their eyes glinted with excitement as they marched, looking forward to accomplish the task set them by the great sage. They walked along the southern bank of the Sarayu and paid their homage to the river.

As the sun went down over the Sarayu, a pastel peach bled into lilac at the horizon. Vishwamitra decided to break journey on the river bank for the night. Following the evening ablutions, the sage initiated Rama and Lakshmana to two potent mantras, 'Bala' and 'Atibala'. "As long as you chant these twin mantras, you will be matchless, invincible against any evil force, in sleep and wakefulness. They will protect you from fatigue, every kind of malady and keep you ever youthful," Vishwamitra explained to them.

Rama and Lakshmana felt happy at having learnt something new. They retired for the day after crafting their beds from straw and dry leaves. As the first stars emerged on a dusky sky, they fell into a well of blissful sleep.

The brothers continued their journey with Vishwamitra the following morning after offering their obeisance to various deities and chanting the Gayatri mantra. All through their way to the sage's ashram, the great seer regaled them with stories galore. Towards evening they came upon the magnificent sight of the confluence of the Ganga and Sarayu. They were enamoured of this spectacular vista and decided to spend their night here.

The trio resumed the passage to their destination the following day. They had to cross the Ganga in order to reach Vishwamitra's ashram. When they reached mid river, the waters turned turbulent with thrashing waves. A tumultuous roar was caused by the gushing waters of the Sarayu as it merged with the river Ganga, known here as river Jahnavi. The princes were amused to hear from Vishwamitra that Ganga was once swallowed in entirety by sage Jahnu because she had inundated his sacrificial ground; later he released her through his ears. She then earned the name Jahnavi, daughter of Jahnu!

Rama and Lakshmana followed Vishwamitra into the dense Dandaka forest after crossing the Ganga. The forest, bereft of proper trails was difficult to negotiate. It was ridden with wild beasts and birds of prey, and filled with a cacophony of terrible, eerie sounds. The jungle was once a prosperous territory, home to the kingdoms of Malada and Karusa.

Tataka

With the passage of time, the prosperous land of Dandaka came to be inhabited by Tataka, a yaksha woman who could assume any form at will. She was born, endowed with the vigour of a thousand elephants. This was because of a boon granted by Brahma to Suketu, her father who begot her after performing severe austerities. When she came of marriageable age, Tataka wed Sunda, the son of demon Jambha. Mareecha was born from the union of Tataka and Sunda. However, when Sunda died because of a curse by sage Agasthya, Tataka sought revenge. When she once spotted the sage, she charged towards him, along with her son Mareecha, to devour him. Agasthya cursed Mareecha to become transformed into an ogre. He then turned to Tataka and said, "May you turn into a hideous man-eating ogre and shed all the goodness associated with a yaksha woman!"

Tataka turned into a cannibal due to Agasthya's curse. She wrecked havoc on Dandaka region and laid waste, an area that was once a place of sylvan beauty.

As they wove their way through Dandaka, Vishwamitra alerted the brothers to be prepared to face the fury of Tataka. Rama rose to the occasion. He strung the bow and twanged it. The entire forest shook and throbbed at the sound caused by the stringing of the bow. Tataka who was now provoked, charged at them, raising a cloud of dust. As Rama hesitated to shoot at a woman, Vishwamitra urged him, "Rama, as a kshatriya and an upholder of dharma, it is your duty to annihilate the dark forces that are a menace to society. By killing Tataka and her army, you will restore Dandaka to its former glory and make it peaceful, prosperous and livable once again."

A fierce fight followed between Rama, Lakshmana and Tataka. She greeted the scions of Ishvaku with showers of rocks. The princes parried these with counter showers. When the demon rushed towards Rama, he chopped off her arms while Lakshmana severed her ears and sliced the tip of her nose. Tataka then made herself invisible and rained stones on the brothers. Rama who was skilled at hitting invisible targets merely by hearing their sounds, made short of his work. His arrow pierced Tataka. She fell down, vanquished.

A crescent moon, graceful and tantalizing as a lady's eyebrow, glowed over Dandaka. It regained its lost glory.

As innumerable stars graced the night sky and the moon bathed Dandaka in its mellow light, Rama and Lakshmana slept, happy to have accomplished yet another feat.

A fragrant dawn breeze gently caressed the brothers and roused them from slumber. Vishwamitra was pleased with the princes for the indomitable courage they had displayed against Tataka, who they killed. He rewarded them by imparting to them knowledge of celestial missiles.

Before they progressed to the last stretch of their journey towards Vishwamitra's ashram, the sage gifted the princes, missiles that could immobilse the enemy, strike at any target, influence the weather and natural phenomena. Vishwamitra also instructed them on how to invoke, use and recall the various weapons.

Siddhashrama

The three of them finally reached Siddhashrama, Vishwamitra's hermitage, where Vishnu had once sat in meditation. Once at the ashram, Vishwamitra began to make serious preparations for the yajna.

The sacrifice was performed day and night over a period of six days while Rama and Lakshmana kept strict vigil at the venue. On the sixth day, as the sacrificial fire blazed at the altar, a loud and fearful uproar rent asunder the air. Dense dark clouds swiftly wafted across the sky, eclipsing the sun. The heavens, space and earth appeared devoid of light. Subahu and Mareecha lunged towards the altar where the yajna was in progress, ready to rain down a deluge of filth. Rama and Lakshmana stopped them in mid air. As Lakshmana was all set to use one of the most potent missiles on Mareecha, Rama advised him against it. He said, "It is not yet time for him to depart from this world. Hence, do not kill him."

Rama then hurled a weapon that struck Mareecha's breast. It did not kill him, but flung him far into the deep ocean and rendered him senseless. Once they dispensed with Mareecha, Rama and Lakshmana slayed Subahu and the rest of the rakshasas who threatened to interrupt the yajna.

Vishwamitra effusively praised Rama and Lakshmana for helping him to successfully conclude the yajna. The erudite assembly of rishis who participated in the sacrifice, applauded Rama. They suggested to Vishwamitra that the brothers accompany their entourage to the kingdom of Videha to witness the sacrifice performed by King Janaka. Vishwamitra concurred with the rishis and embarked on the journey to Mithila, the capital of Videha.

The hermits who began their journey from Siddhashrama to Mithila, stopped to rest on the banks of the Sona for the night. After performing the daily evening worship, they sat down around Vishwamitra under a tree. Rama, enamoured of his surrounds, expressed his desire to know of its origins.

Vishwamitra began to narrate the story of Siddhashrama. "Several ages ago, the region was ruled by royal sage

Kusanabha who performed penance to beget a son. The sacrament bore fruit. My father, the extremely pious Gadhi, was born. Since I hail from the line of Kusa, I am known as Kausika," explained Vishwamitra.

Vishwamitra continued his story and told him that he had a sister by name Satyawati who ascended to heaven after leading a virtuous life. She later turned into the sacred river Kausiki, 'Kosi' of modern times, flowing by the side of the Himalayas.

They were well into the night when Vishwamitra concluded his story. With miles to go the next day, the retinue dropped into a well of sleep.

Rama and the rishis woke up early the following morning, and were greeted by the spectacular sight of River Sona which shone like a glittering sheet of glass. A thin veil of mist wove sinuous patterns on its surface even as the rising giant cast its shimmering glow on its waters. After taking a dip in the river and worshiping the Sun god, the group of men crossed the river and once again entered the forests. As they traversed the jungle trail, the woods reverberated with the joyous cries of a myriad birds swooping and soaring in salute to daybreak. Once again, the rishis came in sight of the Ganga, coursing a long route through the three worlds, negotiating winding pathways through mountains and valleys.

When Rama urged him, Vishwamitra briefly recounted the story of Ganga. Ganga was the daughter of Himavan, the presiding deity of the mighty Himalayas. In order to ensure welfare of the gods who approached him for securing their wellbeing, Himavan gave Ganga to them. Ganga followed a three-course path and first entered the realms of heaven where she was worshipped as Mandakini.

Sagara, a king of Ayodhya and an ancestor of Rama once undertook to perform a sacrifice to propitiate the gods. Unfortunately, he could not bring the yajna to fruition as Indra stole the sacrificial horse. Sagara's sixty thousand sons who went in search of the horse to the subterranean region incurred the wrath of sage Kapila, upon which they turned into mounds of ash. Bhageeratha, the fifth generation of Ikshvaku kings from Sagara, accomplished the task of bringing Ganga down from heaven to wash the ash mounds of Sagara's sons and liberate them from their sins. Thus, Ganga, brought down to earth by Bhagiratha, came to be known as Bhagirathi.

Ahalya

As Vishwamitra's retinue approached the outskirts of Mithila, they came upon an abandoned ashram. The whispering breeze and the breathtaking sylvan forests made it appear like a resort in paradise. The hermitage belonged to sage Gautama who lived here in peace and joy with his wife, the pious Ahalya. Once when the rishi was away from his dwelling, Indra appeared before Ahalya in the guise of her husband Gautama. Ahalya who lost her equanimity for a few fleeting moments, succumbed to his embrace.

Indra who had accomplished the purpose for which he had come, wanted to leave before Gautama returned. Unfortunately for him, Gautama entered his cottage just then and seeing Indra in his guise and guilty of misdemeanor, cursed him. Gautama also cursed his wife Ahalya to become invisible, live on air and continue residing in the ashram without food or water. He then informed her that she would be redeemed from the curse when Rama, the glorious prince of Ayodhya and son of Dasaratha would set foot in their hermitage. Gautama himself, then left for the Himalayas to perform greater austerities.

"Rama, please enter the sacred abode of sage Gautama, for it is now time for Devi Ahalya to be liberated from the curse," said Vishwamitra.

As soon as Rama stepped into the ashram, there was a sudden flash of brightness. Ahalya appeared before them, looking divinely radiant and beautiful. At the same instant, Gautama also returned from the Himalayas. Rama and Lakshmana took the blessings of Ahalya and Gautama before leaving for Mithila.

Mithila

When Vishwamitra entered Mithila with Rama and Lakshmana, its streets were abundantly adorned and preparations for the sacrifice were in full swing. King Janaka, along with his family priest Satananda, the son of Gautama Rishi and Ahalya, welcomed Vishwamitra with due honours.

Satananda made eager enquiries about the his parents' welfare. He was overcome with joy when he heard from Vishwamitra that his parents were united.

Satananda then turned his attention to Rama and the rest of the guests. He extolled the virtues of Vishwamitra and related incidents from his inspiring life. Vishwamitra was born a Kshatriya and began his political life as a mighty ruler. However, he soon tired of this living and turned to perform tapas and austerities. He sought, and earned the coveted honour of being called "Brahmarishi", a title that had hitherto been bestowed only upon sage Vasishta.

When Trisanku, the former king of Ayodhya had wanted to perform a sacrifice so that he could bodily ascend heaven, it was Vishwamitra who helped him achieve this.

As the yajna progressed, Trisanku's ascent to heaven at the sage's command, halted midway by a counter command from Indra. Vishwamitra then created a new galaxy with a group of seven constellations around Trisanku. All the gods concurred, and Trisanku enjoyed heavenly bliss, amidst brilliantly shining stars.

On another occasion, when Vishwamitra's nephew Sunahsepa was tied to a sacrificial pole at a yajna performed by King Ambarisha, the sage taught him mantras to glorify Indra and Vishnu. "Son, chant these mantras. They will deliver you from death and bestow upon you a long life. At the same time, Ambarisha will also get the fruit of his sacrifice by the grace of Indra and Vishnu."

True to Vishwamitra's words, both Sunahsepa and Ambarisha attained their respective goals.

Shiva's bow

Rama and Lakshmana were as keen to know about the origins of the extraordinary bow in Janaka's court, as they were eager to see it. Janaka gave them a lucid account of the its presence in Mithila.

The devas gave Janaka, *Pinaka,* the divine bow of supreme strength and effulgence. It originally belonged to Shiva, who obtained it as a reward for austerities he had undertaken. It was now displayed regally as an object of worship in King Janaka's palace.

King Janaka once desired to perform a yajna. In preparation for the event, he identified an appropriate tract of land. He was ready to plough the plot after observing the associated rites and traditions. Just as he made to dig the earth, he was amazed to see an infant girl lying there in the furrow. When the child heard voices, she gurgled and flashed a beaming smile at Janaka. The king who was irresistibly drawn to the child, picked her up and cradled her in his arms. The monarch and his consort, queen Sunayana, who had no issue, were overjoyed and adopted the baby as their own daughter. They named her 'Sita', meaning 'furrow' in Sanskrit, for the plough trench where she was discovered. Infant Sita brought, fortune to her foster parents. They were soon blessed with their own daughter, Urmila. The sisters grew up in an atmosphere of love, learning and devotion.

When Sita reached adulthood, Janaka sought to have her betrothed and wedded to a groom, compact of all virtues and valour. Several prospective kings and princes sought her hand in marriage. But none was good enough for his Sita. Janaka then placed a condition that Sita would marry the suitor who would string *Pinaka,* the celestial bow in his possession. Many rulers and princes tried their hands at the bow, to no avail.

The bow was yet unstrung when Vishwamitra arrived at Mithila. The sage asked King Janaka to present it before the sons of Dasharatha. Janaka proudly did so. *Pinaka,* draped in all finery, looked magnificent in its iron chest which was mounted on eight wheels. A few hundreds of men dragged the chest to the king's centre court for Rama to see.

Janaka was skeptical about Rama's ability to handle the bow. He addressed Vishwamitra most humbly and respectfully: "Neither gods nor gandharvas, kinnaras, nor yakshas, nagas nor demons, have been able to string this bow. How will a mere mortal as young as Rama be able, even to budge it?"

Vishwamitra, upon hearing Janaka's words, asked Rama to step forward and display his prowess with the bow. Rama strode gallantly towards the chest, and gently but firmly opened it. As he stood before it, mesmerized by its bewitching majesty, the bow appeared to beckon him. There was a hushed silence in the court. Those assembled, waited with bated breath in anticipation. In a single swift, and easy movement, Rama lifted Pinaka. By the mere alchemy of his touch, the bow was not only strung, but it bent and broke in two! The hall echoed with the thunderous sound of the breaking bow. The earth appeared to tremble at the enormity of this feat. A mere lad had performed the impossible. There was loud cheering and applause as Janaka declared Rama as his daughter's groom.

Janaka then dispatched messengers to Ayodhya to acquaint Dasharatha with the happenings at Mithila. He invited the king of Ayodhya to Mithila to solemnize the wedding of Rama and Sita.

The marriage

Dasharatha was ecstatic with the tidings he received from Janaka. Dasharatha, after consulting Vasishta and other sages, prepared to leave for Mithila. Ayodhya was agog with the news of Rama's forthcoming wedding to Sita. The infectious spirit of joy spread rapidly across the city which already wore a festive look.

At daybreak on the following day, Dasharatha, with his queens, Bharata and Shatrugna left for Mithila. A large entourage of sages, counselors, ministers, family and friends, followed him.

Dasharatha and his entourage, were warmly welcomed by Janaka. He and his people were comfortably settled for their stay. The wedding ceremony lasted four days. It began with the introduction of the bride's and groom's lineage. Vasishta narrated the family genealogy on behalf of Dasharatha, while Janaka himself recounted his pedigree.

Dasharatha, through Vasishta, also solicited Urmila's hand for Lakshmana. Janaka was overjoyed to have Lakshmana as the groom for his younger daughter. At the same time, Vasishta and Viswamitra, on behalf of Dasharatha sought Janaka's nieces as life partners for Bharata and Shatrugna. Mandavi and Srutakirti were daughters of Kusadhwaja, the younger brother of King Janaka. The prospect of four wedding celebrations taking place simultaneously caused much jubilation amongst those gathered.

Mithila witnessed a flurry of activity. A grand pavilion was erected for the wedding ceremony. It was draped in a mélange of silk fabric, studded with glistening pearls and gems. Fragrant floral streamers and buntings adorned its pillars and walls. The sweet smell of incense wafted through the air. The vast arena pulsated with excitement as kings and their deputies gathered from various regions of Bharata Varsha. Vedic hymns and chants were recited even as music from an orchestra of instruments added melody to the mirthful atmosphere that prevailed. Gleeful shouts of "Glory to Rama, Glory to Sita" reverberated through the city of Mithila.

Dasharatha approached the sacrificial fire with his four sons. Bejeweled and attired in silken robes, they looked resplendent. When the princes were seated, Sita, followed by her sisters arrived at the pavilion. Sita of slender waist and long black tresses, walked daintily to the dais, her face shining with the luminosity of the moon. Her sparkling eyes danced with joy as she cast secretive looks at Rama. Her sharp features glistened with the brilliant luster of gems. She needed no adornments to accentuate her beauty. Yet, the ornaments of gold, embedded with diamonds and other precious stones that she sported, enhanced her naturally pretty looks.

Dasharatha's sons were captivated by the beauty of their spouses-to-be who looked no less than heavenly beings. The couples, one by one, walked, hand in hand around the ceremonial fire. They took their vows to be man and wife, pledging their togetherness under every circumstance that life would expose them to. The divine beings from heaven, who watched the marriages from above, showered flowers upon the newly-weds.

Following the nuptials, Dasharatha took leave of Janaka and proceeded to return to Ayodhya with his people. Simultaneously, sage Vishwamitra too returned to his hermitage.

Parashurama

As they were returning to Ayodhya, Dasharatha was overcome by a sense of unease because of the ominous signs he perceived. He expressed his concerns to Vasishta who allayed his fears. All of a sudden, dark clouds blanketed the sky and there was a deafening sound. A terrifying tempest uprooted trees and sent wild beasts running amok in bewilderment. Even as Dasharatha and his ministers wondered at nature's sudden fury, an enormous cloud of dust rose, and from it Parashurama emerged. This son of Jamadagni rishi, who looked as fearsome and threatening as ever, blocked their path.

Jamadagni had been unjustly killed by Kartavirya Arjuna, the Kshatriya king with thousand arms. Since then, Parashurama considered all kshatriyas as his enemies. He wiped out the entire clan that he held responsible for his father's brutal and untimely demise. Once Parashurama vanquished all the kings and established his supremacy over them, he retired to the forests of Mount Mahendra to atone for his sins. Now, upon hearing of Rama's prowess with the *Pinaka,* Parasurama rushed from Mount Mahendra to confront him with the Sharanga, Vishnu's bow.

Parashurama, a descendant of Bhrigu, sported matted locks coiled at the crown, and wielded an axe, bow and shaft in his hands. He scornfully looked at Rama, and challenged him, "Oh valiant son of Dasharatha, I just heard of your skills in bending and breaking the Pinaka. I have in my possession an equally mighty bow, that of Vishnu. String it now and prove your might. If you succeed, you would be worthy of a single combat with me!"

Dasharatha who was aghast at these words, appealed to Parashurama's noble birth and scholarly upbringing. He also politely reminded Parashurama of his vows to end his hostilities with the kshatriyas. "Honourable rishi, you renounced all your earthly possessions, turned them over to sage Kashyapa and retired to Mount Mahendra to perform austerities. It is not becoming of you to indulge in combat now."

Parashurama, however, turned a deaf ear to Dasharatha's entreaties and continued speaking to Rama.

"Come on, Rama, I dare you to string this bow!" he thundered.

Rama, who had hitherto remained silent as a mark of respect to his father and other elders around him, responded to the challenge. He seized the bow and arrow from Parashurama's hands and said, "I will not hurl this arrow at you for the twin reasons that, I respect you, and you share kinship with the great Vishwamitra. However, since the arrow has to be discharged once it is removed from its quiver, I place before you, two options. Do I render you immobile with it, or would you rather give up all the merit accrued to you through your austerities?"

Thus saying, Rama strung the Sharanga with a swift movement. All the heavenly beings – Brahma along with the gods, gandharvas, kinnaras, yakshas, siddhas, nagas, ogres and demons, applauded Rama's magnificent feat. Parashurama was rendered speechless. He bowed in reverence before Rama and said, "I surrender to you, the merits of asceticism that I have obtained to far. I am now convinced that you are Lord Vishnu incarnate!"

The veil of darkness surrounding them, lifted. Parashurama circumambulated Rama and left for Mount Mahendra.

Rama returns to Ayodhya

Dasharatha and his men proceeded to Ayodhya. The capital of the Kosala king was awash with colour in preparation to welcome the royal couples. The celebratory sounds of drums, conches, trumpets and cymbals, could be heard for miles before the royal procession reached the city gates. The Kosala capital exploded into a kaleidoscope of colour with the continuous roll of firecrackers. Every lane and alleyway of Ayodhya dazzled with lights, adding glitz and sparkle to the silhouette of temples and buildings.

To such tumultuous greeting, the brides of Dasharatha's sons were heralded into their new home. United in wedlock, the couples enjoyed a blissful life in Ayodhya. They also discharged their duties towards each other, their family and State, with utmost devotion.

All for the crown

Dasharatha's sons soon settled down to life of householders. Kaikeyi's brother Yudhajit, invited his nephew Bharata, to visit Rajagriha, the capital of the Kekaya kingdom. Shatrugna who was Bharata's inseparable companion, accompanied him.

Meanwhile, the ageing Dasharatha wished to hand over the reins of his kingdom to the younger generation. As a first step in this direction he desired to install Rama, his first-born as regent.

Dasharatha's decision was in keeping with royal norms of designating the eldest son as prince regent. In addition, the king fairly adjudged Rama to be most worthy of this station. He turned over in his mind the traits of his eldest son who remained a stoic in the face of life's contrasts. Who could be more worthy than the compassionate Rama who was replete with talents and suave of speech, to continue the Ikshvaku lineage? Was Rama not a valiant and courageous warrior, a votary of truth and righteousness who had mastered the Vedas? Was Rama not unflinching in his devotion to his father, and to the people and kingdom of Ayodhya?

Dasharatha deeply reflected thus, on Rama's worthiness to become prince regent. He then held court with his ministers and counselors. He was delighted that the assembly, in unison, concurred with his decision. Without any delay, as bid by their king, the ministers began preparations for Rama's installation ceremony. While Ayodhya was agog with a flurry of activity to carry out Rama's installation ceremony, Dasharatha became distraught on account of a portentous dream he had. He wished to expedite Rama's coronation. He was also keen to perform the ritual during Bharata's absence from Ayodhya. Dasharatha was certain of Bharata's innate goodness and piety, and was aware of his love for, and loyalty towards Rama. Yet, an element of doubt caused him to feel restless and he argued within himself: "The minds of men are not entirely predictable, they could be unstable." Dasharatha duly conveyed his resolve to his council of ministers and then summoned Rama to his private chamber. The emperor, thereupon asked Rama to observe, along with Sita, the obligatory formalities leading to his ceremonial installation.

Manthara

Ayodhya was bathed in a riot of colours and wore a festive look. The city fibrillated with activity as its citizens prepared to witness the much awaited event. Manthara, Kaikeyi's hunchbacked maid was puzzled at the sudden rush of activity in the capital. She wondered why Kausalya was making generous gifts of wealth to the priests of the kingdom. When Manthara learned the reason for these gestures, she immediately rushed to Kaikeyi. She agitatedly addressed the queen who was relaxing in bed: "Wake up, you innocent woman from your delusions! How can you rest so peacefully when you are in grave danger!"

Kaikeyi was amused at Manthara's outburst and asked her the reason for her anger. Manthara raged, "Do you not see that preparations are afoot to ruin you? Rama is to be installed as Prince Regent tomorrow. The arrogant Kausalya is gleefully distributing gifts to people."

Kaikeyi laughed when Manthara admonished her in this manner. She said, "But these are good tidings that you have brought me. The news of my beloved Rama's forthcoming coronation is a cause for rejoicing!" She further reprimanded Manthara for entertaining unkind thoughts about Rama who loved her and respected her as much as he did his own mother Kausalya. "Who is more deserving of the crown than the virtuous Rama who is the epitome of Truth and Righteousness? Shame on you Manthara, for thinking so unkindly of my dear son!"

But Manthara was unrelenting. "How can you be so naïve, silly woman! Do you not see that the king has played foul in arranging for Rama's installation when Bharata is away! You and your son will now become slaves to Rama and his mother Kausalya once Rama is invested with the office of prince regent! Go, ask the king for what is rightfully yours! Get the throne for Bharata and have Rama banished to the forest for fourteen years!"

Manthara was so forceful in her arguments that she convinced Kaikeyi to covet the throne for Bharata. The seeds of poison sown by the maid took firm hold of Kaikeyi. She asked, "But how do I accomplish this impossible task, Manthara? Is it not the norm and privilege of a king's eldest and worthy son to succeed his father? How then, can I ask for Bharata to be installed as regent?"

Manthara reminded Kaikeyi of the two boons Dasharatha had promised her long ago. A young Dasharatha, in order to help Indra, had once fought a war against the demon Timidhwaja, also known as Sambara. Kaikeyi had accompanied Dasharatha on his chariot. When he fell unconscious after being grievously wounded, she rode his chariot to safety and nursed him back to health. Dasharatha appreciated her timely action and was grateful to her for it. To show his profound gratitude for her admirable deed, he granted her two boons. Kaikeyi had then responded by saying, "I shall ask these boons of you when I need them."

Manthara interrupted Kaikeyi's reverie. "Now is the time for you to hold your husband to his promise. Ensure the crown for Bharata and exile for Rama. Fourteen years is good enough time for Bharata to prevail over the people of Ayodhya and prove his worthiness to them!"

Kaikeyi invokes the boons

Kaikeyi promptly acted upon Manthara's evil counsel. On the eve of Rama's investiture, Kaikeyi strode with determination, to the sulking chamber of the palace. She rid herself of all ornaments, let her hair down in a disheveled state, and slumped down on the floor. Dasharatha who was eager to share the forthcoming event with his favourite queen, came looking for her. He was informed that she had retired to the sulking room in an extremely angry mood. The king was distressed to hear this, and he immediately proceeded to see her. When he saw her lying sprawled on the floor in a distraught state, he begged her to reveal the reason for her sudden sorrow.

Without much fuss, Kaikeyi told him that she now wanted him to grant the two boons he had promised her long ago. An unsuspecting Dasharatha said he would be only too happy to make good his promise. Kaikeyi, unabashedly looked into the king's eyes and made her claims. Dasharatha was stunned into speechlessness. He wondered if he was having a bad dream! When he recovered from the initial shock, he realized it was reality in its most cruel garb. He agonized at the unreasonable demands made by her. He tried to make her see reason and elaborated on Rama's virtues. He reminded Kaikeyi of her own love for Rama and the measure in which Rama reciprocated his affections for her. But Kaikeyi was beyond reason. She was relentless in the pursuit of her goal. She taunted the honourable Ikshvaku descendant for going back on his words.

Dasharatha could not believe his eyes and ears. It seemed incredulous that his beloved queen had assumed such a ruthless and demoniac character. Dasharatha lost his cool and acted like one demented. He raved and ranted, feeling helpless at his plight. He lamented at the misfortune that had suddenly befallen him. He wondered at the evil that possessed Kaikeyi. Neither reason, nor pleading for sympathy moved her. Dasharatha transgressed all bounds of decorum and went down on his knees, pleading with Kaikeyi to be merciful. The queen only spewed more venom, scoffed at him and turned away from his entreaties. Dasharatha collapsed and fell to the floor from sheer exhaustion.

When Dasharatha recovered from the swoon, he rose and wailed at his predicament. "How will I break this terrible news to Kausalya? How will I tell her that I am the reason for the fate that has befallen her dear son? How will I face Sita with such evil tidings? What will I tell the people of Ayodhya who are joyfully preparing for Rama's investiture? How can I bear to send my dear Rama to the forest?"

Dasharatha who was aggrieved and angered by Kaikeyi's unscrupulous demands, alternated between volleying harsh words at her, and beseeching her to show compassion. The old king appeared to have aged several years in a matter of hours. He bemoaned his folly and misfortune in having taken Kaikeyi for his queen, a woman who was so full of bile and venom.

Night gave way to a new dawn, and with it arrived the day of Rama's coronation. Sage Vasishta who was ready to initiate the pre-coronation rituals, asked Sumantra to inform Dasharatha that they must perform the ceremony without further delay as the auspicious time for its conduct, was running out. Dasharatha was still in a state of stupor when Sumantra arrived to convey Vasishta's message. Kaikeyi used this to her advantage and asked Sumantra to summon Rama to her palace because the king desired to see him.

Rama honours his father's promise

Rama who had completed all the pre-installation rituals, left with Sumantra to meet his father. He became apprehensive when he saw Dasharatha's fatigued appearance and distressed look. He bowed to his father and king, with due respect. Dasharatha who had a caged look, stared vacantly at Rama and did not acknowledge his greeting. He had become extremely exhausted by the events of the night and gravity of the situation. He felt so weighed down by guilt, that he could barely look his son to his eyes, or even utter his name.

Rama was unable to comprehend the king's strange behavior which was so uncharacteristic of him. "Why is father looking so agitated? Have I unwittingly offended him that he is so angry with me?" Rama asked Kaikeyi.

Kaikeyi who was already deep in the arms of evil, made a calculated and crafty move upon hearing Rama's words.

She replied, "Rama, he is neither in anguish nor is he angry with you. It is just that in keeping his promise to me, he has to convey unpleasant tidings to you. For an honourable and righteous king, it is not appropriate to go back on his words. I will tell you what ails him, if you are prepared to execute his wish.

Rama who was extremely pained to hear Kaikeyi's words, humbly assured her. "Mother, I feel ashamed that I have given you room for entertaining such doubts about my devotion to father. I would be only too glad even to give up my life at his bidding. His wish is my command. Please tell me what is it that he wishes me to do."

Kaikeyi grabbed the opportunity before her and apprised Rama of the boons and how when he heard her wishes, Dasharatha showed unwillingness to grant them. Rama remained unperturbed by Kaikeyi's revelation, and assured her that, as a dutiful son, he would willingly and happily, honour his father's promise to her. Kaikeyi who was overjoyed to hear this, made sure that Rama would not delay embarking on his journey to the forest.

Dasharatha who had remained silent all this while, gave a weak cry of despair and agony when he heard Rama's words. He fell down unconscious. Kaikeyi remained unmoved. She urged Rama to expedite his move to the woods. Rama gently picked his father up, and before leaving the chamber, spoke to Kaikeyi: "I covet neither the kingdom nor wealth nor the material comforts of this world. I would forever be on the side of Truth and Righteousness. I would go any lengths, even at the cost of my life, to serve my father. Let noble Bharata rule Ayodhya."

Dasharatha was tongue-tied with grief and wept bitterly as Rama departed, to break the news to his mother

Kausalya. The queen mother was devastated when Rama detailed the turn of events to her. She wailed without restraint, and chided her husband for having lost his sense of fairness, for submitting to the unreasonable demands made by Kaikeyi.

Lakshmana was infuriated with the king's conduct and pronouncement. He asked Rama to ignore the biddings of a king gone senile and turned foolish, bullied as he had been, by an evil woman. Lakshmana argued with Rama saying that when situations demanded, it was necessary to go against the wishes and command, even of a father or teacher. "When one fails to distinguish between right and wrong, when one's judgement becomes cloudy and he errs from the path of righteousness, it is only fair that you should not support the cause. Does father have just reasons for stripping you of your right to kingship? What wrong have you done to deserve being banished from Ayodhya?"

Kausalya joined hands with Lakshmana in this tirade against Dasharatha. She too advised Rama against fulfilling Dasharatha's wishes because they merited no worth. Rama remained unwavering in his resolve to carry out his father's promise. He consoled Kausalya and Lakshmana by giving examples of Parashurama, Sage Kandu, and of King Sagara's sixty thousand sons who had discharged with great pride, what their respective fathers had commanded. He also extolled the virtues of righteousness, truth and piety to Kausalya, and sought her permission to leave for the forest.

Rama, who was steady of mind, pacified Kausalya and Lakshmana saying that his expulsion from Ayodhya was destiny driven, and not the handiwork of Kaikeyi or Dasharatha, who were but instruments in fate's hands. Lakshmana, however, refused to accept Rama's explanations. He rebuked him for taking refuge in fate to comply with their father's irrational wish. Lakshmana suggested that Rama should take up arms against injustice and fight for what was right. He said, "Noble brother, you would be doing this in the interests of our people, for the welfare of Ayodhya." The son of Sumitra was all set to fight on behalf of Rama. His voice reflected the intense anger he felt. He said, "Are these weapons in my possession, embellishments to enhance my physical charm! Of what use are they if I cannot deploy them to fight and trounce enemies, dear brother!"

Rama who was determined to honour his father's pledge, fended every plea and admonishment with apt reply. Kausalya realized the futility of arguing with Rama. She, however, begged him to allow her to accompany him to the forest. Rama firmly reminded her of her duty towards Dasharatha. He reiterated that the king needed her support now more than ever, in this dark hour when he felt betrayed by his most cherished wife, Kaikeyi. "If you desert father now, especially after I leave for the forest, he will certainly not survive. You have to be his pillar of support, mother," insisted Rama. Kausalya recognized the finality in Rama's tone and resigned herself to the fact that she would not be able to sway him from his stand. She blessed him and bid him do as he deemed right.

Rama took his mother's blessing and proceeded to inform Sita of the latest developments. Sita who heard out Rama patiently, was equally firm in her resolve.

"My abode is where you dwell – be it here in the palace or in the jungles." Through the tears that welled up in Sita's eyes as she spoke to him, Rama could see the steely determination in those soft, lotus petal-like eyes.

Rama's attempts to convince Sita of the hardships of a nomadic life in the forest, failed to impress her. "What fear would I have in the forest, of the beasts that live in the wild, when I have you, to protect me?" she asked. Sita expressed joy on being given this opportunity to live in the lap of nature, surrounded by mountains, rivers, rivulets, fruit and flower trees and plants, and waking up to ambient sounds produced by the creatures of the jungle. To clinch the matter, Sita even threatened Rama with dire consequences to herself if he did not let her go with him to the forest. Rama gave in, as he did with Lakshmana, who argued that his place was beside his brother at all points of time, no matter where he went.

In preparation for their forest sojourn, Rama and Sita distributed abundant gifts and wealth to the sages and priests of Ayodhya. Then, along with Lakshmana, they went to take leave of Dasharatha and seek his blessings.

Meanwhile, Ayodhya was rife with surmises when its people heard of Rama's exile and Bharata replacing him as prince regent. A pall of gloom descended upon the city. Groups of people gathered in its streets, expressing shock and displeasure at the sudden turn of events. They cast aspersions on Dasharatha and questioned his motives. As Rama and Sita proceeded towards the king's chamber, many of these comments fell on their ears but Rama ignored them. He remained calm and undisturbed unlike Lakshmana who was livid with rage.

Sumantra ushered Rama, Lakshmana and Sita into Dasharatha's chamber. As desired by the king, his queens were also present there. The emperor reproached himself before Rama for succumbing to Kaikeyi's unfair demands. He begged Rama to ignore the vow that Kaikeyi had cunningly extracted from him. However, no amount of coaxing or cajoling deterred Rama from his stance. As Dasharatha embraced his son and wished him well, he fell down unconscious from the grief that pierced his heart like a thousand arrows. All those present, wept uncontrollably as Rama exited from the king's chamber.

Sumantra, Dasharatha's most trusted minister and companion, let loose a volley of unforgiving words upon Kaikeyi. He hoped this would make her change her mind and she would relax her stand on Rama going to the forest. Sumantra admonished Kaikeyi for her dastardly deed and accused her of leading her husband and Ayodhya to doom. The loyal minister, without any reservations, vented his wrath on Kaikeyi. He told her that all the scholars and learned men of Ayodhya would rather follow Rama to the forest than be ruled by the son of a wicked woman.

Sumantra taunted Kaikeyi for following in the vile footsteps of her mother who, even at the cost of her husband's life, was intent on having her whims satisfied! In the presence of those assembled, Sumantra recalled an event that had taken place years ago. Ashwapati, the King of Kekeya and father of Kaikeyi, was granted a boon that allowed him to understand the language of birds and animals. The boon, however, was accompanied by a warning that he would lose his life if he divulged the animals' conversations to anybody. One day when Ashwapati and his queen had retired to bed, the king guffawed loudly on hearing the shrill cry of a distant bird. When Kaikeyi's mother desired to know the reason for the king's laughter, Ashwapati informed her that he would be dead upon revealing the bird's words. The queen was still insistent. The wise king who did not give in to his wife's unreasonable demand, banished her to her parental home.

When Sumantra finished narrating this incident, he begged Kaikeyi, Oh, royal lady, do not bring such disaster upon the righteous Dasharatha and his beloved Rama. Neither of them will go back on the word given to you! Take back your boons and save Ayodhya from calamity."

Kaikeyi remained impervious to Sumantra's entreaties as she had to others. When all good counsel had come to naught, Dasharatha, with a heavy heart asked Sumantra to get the chariot ready to take Rama to the forest. He also told him to assemble a complete army of soldiers, elephants, horses and wealth of every kind to take care of the needs of Rama, Lakshmana and Sita during their stay in the jungles. Hearing the king's instructions to Sumantra, an enraged Kaikeyi flared: "Would you dare give Bharata the kingdom stripped of all its wealth?"

Rama immediately intervened and declined to take anything of value with him, except garments of bark as befitting forest dwellers. He declared, "When I have renounced the kingdom to lead the life of an ascetic in the forest, what use would I have for all these riches?"

Kaikeyi, upon hearing Rama's words, without compunctions, shamelessly handed to the three of them, attires of bark. The queen who had suddenly become heartless, made sure they wore these clothes in preparation for their departure. As the assembly of people gathered in the gynaeceum watched Sita struggle to get into the clothes of bark and Rama help her, they were driven to tears. They were distressed upon seeing their beloved Sita clad in the clothes of a hermitess. They pleaded with her to stay back in Ayodhya. They spoke with disdain of Kaikeyi's villainy and shot hateful glances at her.

Sage Vasishta who had hitherto been silent, was immensely moved by Sita's plight, and condemned

Kaikeyi's behaviour. He chided her for having tricked Dasharatha into making the promise and having brought disgrace to the Ikshvaku family. He warned her that if Sita accompanied Rama to the forest, all of Ayodhya, including Bharata would follow them. He reiterated that Bharata being an honourable prince he would neither comply with his mother's devious desire, nor accept to be coronated in place of Rama.

Paying due respects to the peerless Vasishta, Sita however stood firm in her resolve of accompanying Rama to the forest.

In a voice that reflected his anguish and anger, Vasishta addressed Kaikeyi, "Since it was Rama alone you asked to be exiled, take back from Sita the bark garments you've handed her. As your daughter-in-law, she deserves to be richly decked in silken robes and ornaments. She is of her own accord accompanying Rama. She will go to the forest, with all accessories as befitting her stature!"

Dasharatha experienced insufferable angst as Rama, Lakshmana and Sita prepared to embark on their journey. He ruminated sorrowfully on the sin he must have committed in his earlier birth to beget the present misery. In concurrence with Vasishta's comments, he insisted Sita be given all riches to see her through the rigours of forest life.

The three of them took leave of Dasaratha and the queen mothers, after taking their blessings. Rama grieved only at having to leave his ageing parents in the dusk of their lives. Sumitra advised her beloved son Lakshmana to remain unwavering on the path of dharma. She advised him to look upon Rama and Sita as his parents and take care of them.

Rama leaves for the forest

As the chariot began to move with the threesome seated in it, the citizens of Ayodhya followed, wailing loudly and begging Rama not to go. Dasharatha, Kausalya and Sumitra, tears flowing down their cheeks, stood stunned, rooted to the spot where Rama had sought their blessings. They were still in a state of daze, unable to believe what they were witnessing. Meanwhile the crowd that followed Rama's chariot beseeched Sumantra to ride slow so that they could drink in the splendorous beauty of their Rama for as long as they could.

A dark veil of sadness and tragedy cloaked Ayodhya in its embrace. Whispers berating Dasaratha and his spineless attitude in the face of Kaikeyi's wickedness, were no longer hushed.

Dasharatha was overcome by remorse and became resentful of Kaikeyi. He addressed her, "Oh sinful lady, I curse myself for having wed you, charmed by your beauty. You are no longer my wife. I hereby disown you and will have nothing to do with anyone who associates with you. Should Bharata abide by your evil design and covet the throne of Ayodhya, let him not offer oblations to me after I'm gone from this world." After venting his anger in this manner, Dasharatha refused to stay a moment longer in Kaikeyi's mansion. He asked to be taken to the palace of Kausalya, mother of his darling Rama.

Dasharatha continued to be restless and in delirium. His vision seemed to blank out after he himself had sent away the light of his life, Rama. He sought solace in taking Kausalya's hand. Kausalya herself was in an agitated and tortured state, having been parted from her dear son. She wondered how her Rama who had never experienced pain or suffering of any kind, would live in the jungle among wild beasts and demons of most horrible nature. She could not imagine the delicate and dainty Sita facing the hardships of jungle existence, living like a homeless wanderer. Kausalya, to whom these thoughts were unbearable, mourned her fate. She said, "I am sure to have separated a cow from its calf in my previous birth. Why else would I be so afflicted in this life?"

Sumitra, who was committed to righteousness, lauded Kausalya for having given birth to a son as noble and divine as Rama. She consoled her saying, "There is none more virtuous than Rama who is adored by one and all. Look at the compassionate Lakshmana who is so steadfast in his loyalty to Rama! And Sita, a noble soul of royal heritage, truly stands by her husband, sharing his adversity when she could have enjoyed a life of comfort here! Are the three of them, individuals to be pitied and lamented over? Noble Kausalya, cherish them, for they bring undying fame to the Ikshvaku Dynasty. A mother, whose son is Rama, should have no cause for grief."

Rama halts on the banks of the Tamasa

When Rama observed several elderly people of Ayodhya following their chariot, he alighted from it, and walked, accompanied by Sita and Lakshmana. It was twilight when they reached the banks of the Tamasa River. The men who followed from Ayodhya slept under the trees on the river bank. Lakshmana and Sumantra prepared a bed of leaves for Rama and Sita to rest upon, while they themselves kept guard through the night.

Rama woke up much before sunrise. Those who had followed Rama, fatigued by the previous day's journey, were in deep slumber. Seeing this as the opportune moment to stop them from following him, Rama asked Sumantra to drive the three of them across the Tamasa. He also suggested that Sumantra negotiate turns of the chariot in a manner that would make these people believe Rama had gone back to Ayodhya. Rama's plan worked. While he crossed the Tamasa with Lakshmana and Sita, the citizens of Ayodhya returned to their city.

Ayodhya, the city of joy, was now submerged in sorrow. It looked forlorn, shorn of all beauty. The animosity towards Kaikeyi was distinctly discernible amongst the people. "How can we live in this city without our dear Rama? What work do we have in a place where the sinful Kaikeyi holds sway? Has she not brought ruin upon her husband and a virtuous son like Rama, who are both revered for their sterling qualities?" Such were the ramblings throughout Ayodhya.

Rama meets Guha

Meanwhile, Rama journeyed past various territories of Kosala. Wherever he went, he heard villagers scoff at Dasharatha for buckling under pressure from his vile queen and delivering a boon so completely unfair. Rama walked on, unmindful of these comments. The threesome crossed the borders of Kosala to come upon a kingdom fed by the sacred Ganga. The river snaked its way, hugged by several hill ranges and verdant gardens that were divinely magnificent. The crystal blue waters of the Ganga was adorned with wading ducks, cranes and graceful swans. These aquatic birds flapped their wings rhythmically to the gentle flow of the river, creating their own mellifluous symphony as they caused ripples in its waters. Lotuses, lilies, hyacinths and a host of other flowers carpeted the river in places, even as marine creatures swam in gay abandon.

Rama halted on the banks of the Ganga under the flower-laden Ingudi tree. They were in a principality that was ruled by the tribal chief Guha, a dear friend of Rama. Guha who heard about Rama's arrival in his land, rushed to see him and extended all hospitality to the royals. He had a feast prepared for them which Rama politely declined. He favoured a simple meal of fruits and roots as appropriate for ascetics practicing austerities. As night fell, Lakshmana, Sumantra and Guha kept watch while Rama and Sita slept peacefully. Lakshmana spent the night relating to Guha, the events leading up to Rama's exile.

Rama rose early and prepared to travel deeper into the forest after crossing the Ganga. As he made to leave with Lakshmana and Sita in the boat that Guha had got ready, he asked Sumantra to return to Ayodhya. Sumantra turned bleary eyed at having to part from Rama. He expressed dismay at having to henceforth live in a kingdom largely controlled by Kaikeyi who had become vicious and evil. Rama, however, beseeched Sumantra to take care of his father and all his mothers, treating them with equal respect during his absence.

Sumantra was woeful and pleaded with Rama, "How do I return without you, with an empty chariot to Ayodhya? Allow me Rama, to ride the chariot for you and accompany you on this forest sojourn as your constant companion along with Lakshmana and Sita."

Rama responded, "Sumantra, the Ikshvakus have had no greater friend than you. My father needs you now more than anyone else. Impress upon the grieving king and my mother that we are not perturbed or unhappy at having to live in the forest. It is important that you return to Ayodhya and tell mother Kaikeyi to rest assured that I indeed, dwell now in the forest! Without any fears, let her peacefully install her son, and my noble brother, Bharata as prince regent. In this manner the honour of my good father will be vindicated."

Rama took leave of Guha and Sumantra and set sail across the Ganga. Since leaving Ayodhya, it was the first night that the threesome spent all by themselves, in Vatsa, the region between the Ganga and Yamuna rivers. As night drew its dark shroud around them, they retired to bed with heavy hearts. Rama became restless and despaired over his father's angst. He worried that Dasharatha would not survive the catastrophe that had struck him. He feared that his mothers Kausalya and Sumitra would be persecuted by the ruthless Kaikeyi. Rama voiced all these fears to Lakshmana and asked him to return to Ayodhya to save their mothers from Kaikeyi who had become despicable. Rama stewed in self-recrimination, and rued that he was of no use as a son to his mother, the vulnerable Kausalya.

Lakshmana consoled Rama but remained firm on not returning to Ayodhya. "Today I do not wish to be in the company of anyone, not even father, mother or our younger brothers. For that matter I do not even aspire to see heaven without you, dear brother!" With finality in his tone, Lakshmana sealed the subject of being parted from Rama.

With the break of dawn, the trio resumed their journey through the forests. Towards sunset they reached the hermitage of Bharadwaja in the region of the confluence of Ganga and Yamuna. The sage who was aware of Rama's banishment from Ayodhya, welcomed them cordially. He played the hospitable host, and made certain that they were suitably fed and well rested. The threesome heeded Bharadwaja's advice and left for Chitrakoota the next day after seeking the sage's blessings. Before their departure from his ashram, the kindly seer, with the warmth and concern of a father, performed religious rites to ensure their safe onward journey.

To Chitrakoota

Sita was in raptures as they walked towards Chitrakoota hill which was a carpet of emerald. It was replete with tall trees, dense with foliage in various shades of green. They dripped blossoms in medley hues and bowed down humbly towards Mother Earth, laden with juicy fruits. The twittering of birds and call of crickets was music to the travelers who basked in nature's glory without feeling the tedium of walking on thorny pathways. Rama, enamoured of the enchanting environs of Chitrakoota, decided to make this place their home. He had Lakshmana build them a hut. In no time, Lakshmana erected a cozy cottage made from leaves and logs obtained from the forest.

Sumantra learned from Guha that Dasharatha's sons and Sita, had made Chitrakoota their home. Since his mind was put to rest on receiving these tidings, he returned to Ayodhya. The residents of Ayodhya, still melancholic from the recent happenings, wailed when they noticed Sumantra return without their Rama. Even Nature in the city seemed to be in bereavement. Water bodies had cried themselves dry; plants and trees shed their green drape and looked withered. Birds and beasts no longer made ambient sounds and the forests around the Kosala capital were plunged in deathly silence.

Ayodhya plunged in grief

Ayodhya was in the grip of an unnatural and disquieting calm as Sumantra entered its gates. He directly proceeded to the king's palace to deliver Rama's message to

Dasharatha and his wives. The king had many questions for Sumantra. He wanted to know how his beloved child was adjusting to forest life, how the dainty and graceful Sita who was used to royal life walked the jungle path of bramble and bushes, how they slept, what they ate. The questions were as endless as the copious tears that gushed down from his now, ever-moist eyes.

When Sumantra conveyed Rama's message to him, Dasharatha was overcome with more grief. He rued his lack of prudence in granting Kaikeyi the boons. He deplored his recklessness in not having consulted his ministers and well-wishers before sending Rama away. Kausalya who was just as devastated, fainted as Sumantra communicated the sentiments Rama had expressed for his parents. Both, Dasharatha and Kausalya repeatedly begged Sumantra to take them to see Rama in the forest.

Kausalya, unable to bear separation from Rama, taunted Dasharath for the misery he had brought upon them. "Oh king, you who are known for your compassion and kindness, did you not stop to think for a moment, the dire suffering your sons and the young Sita will face in the jungle? A woman's husband and sons are her prime pillars of support, and you have mercilessly robbed me of both, in my old age. How can I lean on you when you are completely under Kaikeyi's spell? My son, my Rama in whom I would find solace, you have driven him away to face a harsh life. Being wed to you, I cannot leave you to go and live with Rama in the forest. You have so completely destroyed me. You have not only ruined me, but also Ayodhya, and entire Kosala!"

Dasharatha winced at Kausalya's sharp words. Their sting was worse than even the sharpest of weapons.

Dasharatha thought to himself: Is it not true that one reaps the fruits of one's own actions, good or bad? Had he not caused unendurable pain to old and infirm parents when he was young? Dasharatha was haunted by the memory of an incident that had occurred when he was prince regent. He unburdened himself to Kausalya as he felt weighed down by it.

Old curse come true

Dasharatha had always been a skilful hunter. He could take aim with his bow at a beast merely by identifying the direction from which sounds emerged, without actually sighting the animal. Once he went out hunting towards the banks of the Sarayu, on a dark night after rains had lashed the forest. The jungle was completely silent. Dasharatha waited for the animals to come out to drink water. Soon he heard a gurgling sound. He believed it to be a creature drinking water. He took aim and hit his target. He was shocked and dismayed when he heard a human voice scream in pain. "Who can be my enemy? Why does he wish to kill me? How will I take this pitcher of water to my old and blind parents? How will they bear to hear of my death?"

Hearing this piteous wail, Dasharatha immediately ran in the direction of the voice. He was appalled to see a young ascetic lying in a pool of blood, pierced by the arrow he had shot.

"I am Shravan Kumar," the young boy revealed to Dasharatha. "I live here with my blind parents. Oh prince, guardian and protector of people, you have caused me grievous injury. I came here to fill water for my aged parents who are thirsty. They would be waiting for me in our ashram. Please give them this pitcher."

Dasaratha was filled with remorse for his hasty and careless action. He slumped down beside Shravan Kumar and begged his forgiveness.

"Please remove this arrow from my body and relieve me of the throbbing ache I feel. Inform my parents of my death at your hands," Shravan Kumar pleaded as he lay bleeding and in intense pain.

The young prince gently pulled the arrow out. Shravan Kumar breathed his last.

Dasharatha was overcome by sorrow and guilt at what he had done. As directed by the dying youngster, he went to the ashram and gave Shravan's parents the water. He confessed his deed to them. The old couple was inconsolable and saddened at their young son's untimely and unnatural death.

"Take us to the spot where our son lies cold," they told Dasharatha.

The mortified prince escorted them to the riverside. The pair cried over Shravan's body, blessed him and performed his last rites. "You too will endure grief after being parted from your son in your old age. You will experience the anguish you have now caused us!" Shravan Kumar's parents cursed Dasharatha with these words before they departed from this world.

"Kausalya, my sin has followed me today. It is killing me now. It is the curse of that blind old couple that has brought this unbearable grief upon me." Dasharatha sobbed, as he related this past event to his wife.

Reminiscing the episode did not relieve the roller-coaster of emotions that Dasharatha was now experiencing - guilt, intense pain and torment. He felt completely shattered, heartbroken and disconsolate. He mumbled to himself, incoherent, incongruous words, as one demented. He called out "Oh Rama, Oh Lakshmana, Oh Sita ... " Night fell and at some time in its dark hours, life ebbed out of the great Ikshvaku king.

The people of Ayodhya woke up to a gloomy dawn. Dasharatha was gone. The kingdom was without a ruler.

Bharata's dreams

Dasharatha's body was duly preserved in a trough of oil for his sons to perform his last rites. Sage Vashishta sent word for Bharata and Shatrugna to return to Ayodhya from Kekaya. He instructed the messengers not to convey the news of Dasharatha's demise to the brothers. He also advised them against referring to the recent events in Ayodhya leading to Rama's exile.

At Kekaya, meanwhile, Bharata woke up in cold sweat from a nightmare he had in the wee hours of the morning. The visions that he had seen were foreboding. He dreamt of his father falling off a mountain peak. He beheld in his dream, several other sights that seemed to warn him of impending disaster.

Bharata's apprehensions gathered volume when he saw men from Ayodhya approaching Rajagriha. As soon as they entered the king's court and handed over the presents from Ayodhya, Bharata anxiously enquired after the welfare of each member of his family. Bharata who was only too familiar with his mother's nature, asked after her welfare in the following words: "How is my mother Kaikeyi, of headstrong disposition and violent temperament, who is ever bent on having her whims and fancies satisfied?" The messengers answered Bharata's questions, respectfully, without divulging, even in small measure, the haps in Ayodhya. They then asked him to immediately return to their capital, to dispense with urgent work there.

Bharata returns to Ayodhya

Bharata and Shatrugna took leave of their uncle and speedily returned to Ayodhya. Bharata felt very uneasy as he approached the city. The air seemed heavy with sadness. He did not see the characteristic mirthful crowd on its streets. As he entered the city through its Victory Gate, he noticed the mournful look on people's faces.

"Why Shatrugna, do our people appear so silent and sad? The musical instruments are not playing! Ayodhya seems to be rid of all joy; nothing looks as it should. I am worried that some misfortune has befallen our kingdom," Bharata expressed his anxiety to his brother.

Bharata saw signs of calamity everywhere. He was unable to contain himself. As soon as the chariot stopped at Dasharatha's palace, he rushed in to meet his father. He became more nervous when he did not see the king in his chamber. He immediately hurried to his mother's palace.

Kaikeyi greeted Bharata with great joy. She hugged him and said, "Oh worthy son, I hope you had a comfortable journey? How are your uncle and grandfather? What news have you brought for me from my parental home?"

Though Bharata was impatient to see his father and learn of his wellbeing, he patiently answered Kaikeyi's barrage of questions. "Everyone is well there, mother. But why is father not to be seen anywhere? The couch upon which he so regally sits, is vacant now! His attendants seem so devoid of their usual gaiety. I must see father now and pay my respects to him," Bharata said. His voice reflected the anxiety and trepidation he felt.

Bharata felt the world crash upon him when Kaikeyi informed him of Dasharatha's demise. He looked at his father's empty bed and broke down, uncontrollable tears streaming down his face.

As Bharata fell on his knees and grieved for his father, Kaikeyi, a picture of nonchalance, spoke to her son, "The kingdom of Ayodhya is now yours to rule! It is not becoming of a king to mourn in this manner. Get up, my son and prepare yourself to accept the glory that is coming your way. You should uphold dharma and follow in the steps of your father and forefathers."

Bharata was now acquainted with all that had transpired in Ayodhya during his absence. He was stunned at the monstrosity of his mother's deed. When he recovered from the state of shock, he was filled with sadness and anger. He exploded at Kaikeyi, livid with rage,

"I am ashamed to call you my mother. You have caused my father's death. You have sinned by sending my most pious and noble brother to the forest. How could you even think of acting in such a despicable manner? Did Rama not always love you and respect you like his own mother? How could you entertain such heinous thoughts for one, who the whole world loves and admires, for one so full of virtues? Do you not know that I love Rama and look upon him as a father? How could you ever imagine that I would be happy robbing him of the kingdom that justly belongs to him? How could you believe that I would have enthroned myself upon my father's grave and enjoy a seat that has been usurped from my brother? Mother, you have paid a very heavy price for a throne that I would not ever bother to covet. I would be eternally happy to serve Rama, as my father and king. You have rendered me fatherless, made widows of mothers Kausalya and Sumitra and orphaned the glorious Kingdom of Kosala by killing its ruler. You, whom I loathe to call my mother, are a curse on my very existence. You have indeed brought ignominy upon me. How do I wash this sin committed by you, off myself?"

Kaikeyi was unperturbed by her son's outburst. She justified her actions. Bharata, however, made it amply clear to her that he would not be party to her evil designs. A single thought was all-pervasive in his mind. He wanted to beg Rama for his forgiveness and bring him back to Ayodhya. He wished to restore to him the throne of Ayodhya which was rightfully his.

Bharata strode out of Kaikeyi's chamber, seething with, sorrow and shame. Along with Shatrugna, he went to meet mother Kausalya in her palace. Kausalya, whose mental faculties were clouded by deep grief, lambasted Bharata with scathing remarks as he approached her. She accused him of perpetrating the tragedy that had befallen her. With sarcasm-laden words, she asked him to ascend the throne that he desired.

Kausalya's sharp words stung Bharata. He fell at her feet and sobbed like a child, denying all knowledge of his mother's dishonourable intentions. Bharata sought to convince Kausalya of his innocence. He assured her he had no role to play in the plot that his mother had hatched. He said, "Mother, if indeed I have sinned, let me suffer the consequences. But what greater punishment could I beget than what I already endure! I have lost my dear father to death; my brother Rama, who I cherish as a father, has been banished. Ayodhya and the world would despise me and hold me accountable for the tragedy that is upon us!"

Kausalya was moved to tears by Bharata's earnest words. She was convinced of the purity of his heart and honesty. Kausalya felt remorse for her verbal attack on him. She gathered him in her arms as she would a child, and consoled him.

Bharata took leave of Kausalya. He informed her of his decision to seek Rama out in the forest and bring him back to be crowned king of Ayodhya.

Bharata, under the guidance of Vasishta, completed the funeral rites of his father. Though he was impatient to seek out Rama and get him to return to Ayodhya, he had to await the conclusion of the thirteen-day mourning period. He completed all ceremonial precepts for the departed king in keeping with scriptural prescriptions. Once the obsequies were discharged, Dasharatha's ministers requested Bharata to assume the throne of Ayodhya. They impressed upon him, that an empire without a ruler would always face the threat of invasion by enemies. Bharata declined all entreaties. He did not relent even at Vasishta's instance that he should assume office of king. He stood firm by his words that Rama alone was the lawful claimant to the kingship of Ayodhya. Bharata compared Rama to the two most illustrious kings of the solar dynasty – Dileepa and Nahusha. He emphasized that Rama alone was worthy of being king. The nobles, ministers, learned men and people of Ayodhya hailed Bharata and lauded the nobility inherent in him.

In the meantime, Shatrugna reflected on the happenings at Ayodhya when they were away at Keykaya. He wondered at the chain of catastrophic events let loose by the urgings and evil counsel of one woman – Manthara. He was puzzled that even the straight-talking Lakshmana could not prevail upon their father to desist from banishing Rama from the kingdom. An avalanche of razor-sharp words tumbled out from Shatrugna's mouth when he spotted Manthara amidst other maids, bedecked in all finery. With the ferocity of a wild beast, he dragged Manthara by her hair and whirled her around in anger. Kaikeyi who witnessed this scene, surmised that she might be Shatrugna's next target. She fled from there to protect herself from his wrath.

Bharata calmed Shatrugna and told him that he himself would have slayed Kaikeyi, but for Rama. He said, "Forgive her, brother. Do you think Rama would ever pardon us or speak to us if we killed Kaikeyi or even this hunchback! Let us, without further delay, depart to the forest to bring back Rama."

Bharata's love for Rama

Sumantra had got the chariots ready for the journey. Bharata left for the forest with a large retinue, comprising the people of Ayodhya, the queen mothers and an army of soldiers, chariots, horses and elephants. Her son's verbal arrows finally brought Kaikeyi to her senses. She too joined Bharata's convoy to bring back Rama.

As dusk was drawing close, the procession reached Guha's principality on the bank of the Ganga. Guha, who saw Bharata approach his region with a huge army, anticipated trouble. He suspected Bharata's intentions and presumed he was here to harm Rama. Guha asked his guards to remain vigilant and watch Bharata's moves. He took further precautions to ensure all defense measures were in place should Bharata attack his territory. Guha then proceeded to meet Bharata, taking with him fruits and sweets to offer to the prince.

Sumantra who observed Guha coming towards them with a large group of attendants, acquainted Bharata with the chieftain's friendship with Rama. He also recounted to Bharata, the great warmth and affection that Guha had showered upon Rama when they had halted a night in his land. Bharata was overjoyed to hear Sumantra's words and now yearned, more than ever, to meet Guha. Once pleasantries were exchanged, Guha described to Bharata the interactions he had with Rama and Lakshmana during their very brief stay at his place. He eulogized Lakshmana's reverence towards Rama and the extreme devotion and love he had for him. He told Bharata about the night-long vigil that Lakshmana had kept over Rama and Sita while they peacefully slept. Guha expressed his distress on seeing the princely Rama and Lakshmana wear garments of bark and sport matted locks like ascetics. With moist eyes, Guha told Bharata, "Sons of Dasharatha who were accustomed to silken couches, had slept under trees, on hard ground upon beds made of grass and leaves."

Bharata felt deep anguish and was driven to tears as Guha described the plight of his dear brothers and Sita. He felt himself responsible for their state of deprivation. He rued his misfortune in not being able to serve Rama, and admired Lakshmana and Sita for standing by him in his adversity. Bharata instantly decided that he too would henceforth, sleep on a bed of leaves and have his tresses matted like hermits. He desired to serve the exile in place of Rama and thereby honour the promise made by his father to Kaikeyi. He wished to see Rama return to Ayodhya and take on the reins of sovereignty.

As twilight merged into night, Bharata slept at the very spot on the banks of the Ganga where Rama had rested. At the break of dawn, with the help of Guha's men, Bharata and his procession crossed the river to sage Bharadwaja's ashram. They took directions from the seer and continued on their way to Chitrakoota to see Rama.

Brothers meet

At Chitrakoota, Sita and Rama enjoyed the bounty of Nature in the midst of which they lived. As they sat soaking in the beauty of their surrounds, Rama observed a cloud of dust being raised at a distance. It was attended by a loud cacophony of sounds. He asked Lakshmana to ascertain the source of the clamour. When Lakshmana noticed the Kovinda tree, the ensign of Ayodhya, fluttering atop the chariots, he guessed that Bharata headed the convoy. Like Guha, he too suspected foul play by Bharata. He believed Bharata had followed Rama to the forest to ensure that he gained undisputed sovereignty of Ayodhya. Lakshmana was ready to fight him. He communicated his thoughts to Rama as he informed him of Bharata's arrival at Chitrakoota with a vast army.

Rama allayed Lakshmana's fears saying, "Lakshmana, do not attribute such uncharitable thoughts to him. Do you not know our Bharata? He knows the way of dharma. It is not to fight or kill that he comes here. He is here to give me back the kingdom. One word from me, and Bharata would even give up his life for me! " said Rama.

On hearing Rama's words, Lakshmana cringed with shame for having entertained such ignoble thoughts of Bharata.

While Rama and Lakshmana were engaged in conversation, Bharata, along with Shatrugna, Guha and Sumantra, approached their cottage. Bharata, who could no longer contain his anxiety and eagerness to meet Rama, had left his army behind, by the banks of the river. Rama came out from the cottage to meet his brother. When Bharata beheld Rama attired in the garb of a recluse, he broke down and fell at his feet, bathing them in a deluge of tears. He begged Rama's forgiveness and asked him to return home and assume the throne of Ayodhya. "I stand condemned for this cruelty that my mother has wrought on you, Mother Sita and Lakshmana. Hell alone is the place for Kaikeyi on whose account we suffer this fate. Come back, noble brother and lift Ayodhya from doom."

Rama was happy to see Bharata. The brothers embraced one another, even as tears choked their voices and they were unable to articulate coherent words. Rama who was full of anxiety about their father, enquired about Dasharatha. Rama fainted on hearing of his demise. Copious tears streamed down his face when he recovered. Lakshmana and Sita were just as inconsolable. They took a dip in the river and offered oblation to the departed king. Rama, as a minstrel dwelling in the forest, could only offer the sacred water of the Mandakini, and balls made from the crushed pulp of the Ingudi fruit to the spirit of his late father.

Soon, Vasishta arrived at Rama's hut, accompanied by Dasharatha's queens and the rest of their entourage. The queen mothers were happy to see their sons. At the same time, it was heart wrenching for them to behold the beautiful Sita bereft of royal trappings. If Kausalya was proud of Janaki's steadfast loyalty to Rama, she was equally pained to see the daughter of Janaka suffer the rigours of forest life alongside her son.

Bharata repeatedly implored Rama to return. He refused kingship of Ayodhya, citing appropriate reasons for doing so. "The throne is neither rightfully mine, nor do I possess your capabilities to rule the land," he said. While he expressed disdain and resentment towards Kaikeyi for the villainy she had engaged in, Bharata did not spare the dead king either. "It is my adherence to morality and kshatriya dharma that prevents me from slaying my mother. I condemn her loathsome act and the dreadful wrong she has done you. I mourn the loss of father. Though I do not desire to speak ill of him, his infatuation for Kaikeyi has led him to his doom. He did not use the judiciousness of his office before banishing you from Ayodhya. He perpetrated a sinful deed only to please a woman. This is not in keeping with the piety, virtue and wisdom for which he was known and loved."

Rama tried to pacify Bharata, explaining that death is man's constant companion that ever stalks him. He urged Bharata to stop grieving for Dasharatha who he said had ascended to heaven after having lived a full and virtuous life. Rama also revealed to him that Dasharatha had been compelled to crown Bharata prince regent because of the promise he had made to Ashwapati, the King of Kekaya at the time of his wedding to Kaikeyi. Rama refuted the aspersions Bharata cast on their father. He explained that the king was bound by his sense of gratitude to Kaikeyi. "Had she not saved him when he was critically injured during the encounter with the demons?" asked Rama. He countered every argument that Bharata laid before him. Rama asked his brother to return to Ayodhya and discharge his duty towards the kingdom and its people.

Bharata asks for Rama's sandals

When Bharata failed to sway Rama from his stance with his arguments, he threatened fast unto death if his brother did not return home and assume kingship of Ayodhya. Even this did not move Rama to budge from his resolve. Bharata realized the futility of his efforts, and agreed to return to Ayodhya. He however, placed before Rama a pair of wooden sandals and asked him to step into them. He informed Rama that he would place the sacred pair on the throne of Ayodhya, as a symbol of Rama's kingship. "I will reside in Nandigrama on the outskirts of Ayodhya and rule the land on your behalf till you return from exile."

Before leaving for Ayodhya, Bharata made a vow in the presence of all those gathered. "If Rama fails to return to Ayodhya on the appointed day upon completion of the fourteen years of exile, I will immolate myself."

In keeping with his word, when Bharata got back to Ayodhya, he placed Rama's sandals on the throne. "Rama is our king," he told its people. "He is away to honour the promise made by our father. He will return at the end of fourteen years and assume this throne which justly belongs to him. Until then, as his servant, I shall bear the responsibility of protecting you, the citizens of this kingdom."

Bharata stayed in Nandigrama and ruled the kingdom with the assistance of able ministers.

Rama leaves Chitrakoota

Rama began to be haunted by the memory of Bharata and his family at Chitrakoota. He felt nostalgic as he recalled their conversations and ached to be with them. He agonized at parting from them once again. He could not remain in Chitrakoota where the memories of his loved ones, rekindled his longing for them. He decided to seek another place in the forest and make it their home. Rama also remembered the promise he had made to the rishis who had fled from the vicinity of Chitrakoota. He had assured them that he would deal with the demons who were terrorizing them, and make the forest safe to live. Hence, along with Sita and Lakshmana, he left Chitrakoota. As they walked, they came upon the ashram of sage Atri and his wife Anasuya. The trio partook of sage Atri's hospitality and upon his advise, moved on to Dandaka forest where they made their new home.

Forest life

Rama, Lakshmana and Sita entered the depths of the Dandaka forest which was infested with wild animals. Here they were confronted by Viradha, a cannibal of enormous proportions. He pounced on Sita and claimed that he would make her his wife. While Rama wallowed in self-pity on seeing Viradha grabbed Sita, an angry Lakshmana geared himself to fight the ogre. In an earsplitting voice, Viradha asked to know the identity of the threesome. Viradha was in reality, Tumburu, a gandharva who had incurred the wrath of Kubera and was therefore transformed into a monstrous ogre. When Tumburu pleaded for mercy, Kubera told him that he would be liberated from his curse when he would meet Rama and be killed by him.

A duel ensued between Viradha and the sons of Dasharatha. The brothers axed the rakshasa's arms. They then dug a pit and buried Viradha in it. The demon was freed from his curse and felt fortunate in having met his end at Rama's hands. However, before life ebbed out of him, Viradha cautioned Rama about the dangers lurking in Dandaka. He directed Rama to meet sage Sarabhanja.

Sarabhanja had patiently waited for the auspicious moment when Rama would step into his hermitage. As destined, the sage shed his mortal coils upon seeing Rama, and ascended to heaven. As advised by Sarabhanja, Rama called on Sage Sutikshana who invited him to make his ashram their abode. Rama who had taken it upon himself to protect the rishis of the forest from the demons, politely declined Sutikshana's offer and continued to roam the various areas of Dandaka.

Sita, however, was apprehensive of Rama taking up weapons to vanquish the evil spirits in the forest. But Rama, who had vowed to help the sages, dispelled Sita's fears. He reminded her that it was his duty as a kshatriya, to protect those who sought refuge in him.

Rama meets Agasthya

Rama visited sages in several ashrams in Dandaka. He now desired to meet the great sage Agasthya who lived deeper south in the forest. Agasthya was a very wise and learned seer who was renowned for his exceptional spiritual powers.

"Sita, do you know how mighty sage Agasthya is? All the rishis went to Mount Kailash to attend the wedding of Shiva and Parvati. But sage Agasthya alone stayed in the south to maintain the balance of the earth!" Rama explained.

"Once, the Vindhya Mountain grew so tall as to reach the skies. It threatened to block the movement of the sun. The gods sought the help of Agasthya," Rama continued to recount Agasthya's various feats, as Sita and Lakshmana listened to him in rapt attention.

"Sage Agasthya then stood in front of the towering mountain which bowed before him in reverence. Agasthya blessed Vindhya with the words, "May you always remain in this form." His words were prophetic. The mountain remained bowed, and stopped growing in height.

On their way to Agasthya's ashram, Rama, Lakshmana and Sita stopped for a while at his brother's hermitage. Agasthya's brother received them cordially and narrated to them the story of the rakshasa brothers Vatapi and Ilvala. The fearsome ogres who were capable of assuming any form, terrorized the rishis dwelling in Dandaka, and killed many of them. Ilvala would assume the form of a learned Sanskrit scholar and invite other erudite men to partake of ceremonial food. Ilvala would use his magical powers to transform Vatapi into a goat. He would then kill the goat, cook it and feed its meat to the unsuspecting seers. When the rishis had partaken of the meal, Ilvala would call out to Vatapi to come out. Vatapi would then emerge, tearing apart, the bodies of the sages. But Agasthya put an end to the demons. When the wicked Ilvala served him the meal, Agasthya consumed it saying, "Vatapi, be digested." When Ilvala called out to his brother, there was no response as Vatapi had been digested by the rishi!

Rama took leave of Agasthya's brother after expressing gratitude for the warmth he accorded them. Agasthya's sanctuary was enchanting with abounding greenery in the midst of which herds of spotted deer, danced. As the three of them stood lost in their surrounds, the sage came out to welcome them. When his guests had partaken of their meal, were well rested, and ready to leave, Agasthya blessed them and presented Rama with divine weapons. He advised them to spend the remaining years of their exile at Panchavati, a safe haven and place of charming beauty that Sita was sure to enjoy.

Rama, along with his brother and consort, headed in the direction of Panchavati, as suggested by Agasthya. On their way they stumbled upon Jatayu, the giant vulture. Lakshmana mistook the creature to be an ogre in disguise. The aged and wise bird sensed Lakshmana's apprehension. He approached the brothers and introduced himself as Dasharatha's dear friend. He also told them that he and his sibling Sampati were the sons of Aruna, and the nephews of Garuda. The threesome were happy to find a friend in the forest.

Panchavati

As they walked the trail canopied by emerald trees, the tranquility of their environs was broken only by the shrill call of birds. Soon they reached Panchavati and were immediately struck by its sublime beauty. They had entered an enchanting world that was a vast palette in shades of green, intermingled with blossoms in motley colours.

"Lakshmana, this place looks so wonderful. We are surrounded by hills that are so lush with trees," said Rama, looking around.

"Look at the sparkling blue waters of the gentle Godavari and the glistening white sands on its banks. Oh, look there, so many deer frolicking with joy!" enthused Sita. She was mesmerized by the acrobatics of the birds. They swooped down upon the lakes one moment, soared high and wheeled in circles through the sky the next moment. She was captivated by this avian drama that unfolded before her. She warmed to the ambient sounds produced by the creatures of the forest.

"Lakshmana, why don't you look for a suitable place and build us a little ashram here?" asked Rama.

Lakshmana at once set about gathering material to construct their home. With great speed and deftness, he raised mud walls and covered the roof with thatch. They settled down to a cozy existence in their new dwelling.

They spent ten happy years in the forest, living in harmony with nature.

The woodland had plenty of ponds that were filled with red, pink, yellow and white lotuses. Their broad green leaves carpeted the water. To Sita, the flowers seemed to rise majestically above the muddy waters of the pond. As the rays of the sun fell gently on them, the lotuses slowly opened up and spread their petals in layers.

Rama, Lakshmana and Sita enjoyed the jet sprays of water from the thundering waterfalls in the forest. The chirping and chatter of birds soothed their ears. Sita loved running after the nimble-footed deer in the woods and watch peacocks dance with their brilliantly-coloured feathers wide open.

Seasons changed, each bringing with it, its unique beauty. The exiled members of Dasharatha's family lived happily nestled in the lap of nature.

Soorpanaka

One day as the brothers and Sita were engaged in mirthful banter outside their ashram, a beautiful young woman approached them and addressed Rama. "Who are you? You look like an ascetic but carry weapons like a warrior."

Rama introduced himself, Sita and Lakshmana to the charming lady who then revealed her true identity to them.

"I'm Soorpanaka, sister of Ravana, the Lord of Lanka. Two of my other brothers in Lanka, have distinguished themselves. While Kumbhakarna is known for his extraordinary strength, Vibhishana is renowned and respected for his wisdom. Khara is another of my brothers and he rules Janasthana region of Dandaka forest. Dooshana, one of my younger brothers, helps Khara."

Soorpanaka was struck by Rama's effulgent beauty and overcome by passion and desired to make him her husband. Soorpanaka who looked ugly with her deformed eyes, crooked nose and enormous belly, was endowed with magical powers. She used this ability to transform herself into a beautiful woman to attract Rama.

"Everyone in this forest is afraid of me. But the moment I set eyes on you, I fell in love with you," she said, her voice filled with arrogance.

Soorpanaka pointed towards Sita, and said, "Leave this chit of a girl and marry me. I am the one worthy of you!"

Rama and Lakshmana teased Soorpanaka, each pointing to the other as being more suited to be her groom. The demoness was enraged when the borthers poked fun at her. She charged ferociously at Sita and threatened to kill her. Lakshmana immediately rose to Sita's defense. He pulled out his sword and chopped off Soorpanaka's ears and nose! She howled wailed in pain as she regained her original form, and rushed out of Panchavati, blood oozing from her wounds. She burst in upon Khara's court, feeling outraged and insulted.

"Brother," she thundered! "Look what the sons of Dasharatha have done to me! Go at once and kill them."

Khara and Dooshana annihilated

Khara initially sent some of his men to fight Rama and Lakshmana. Rama easily overpowered these ogres and killed them. Khara who was livid with fury, summoned Dooshana and along with a huge army, marched to Panchavati to fight Rama. His men, who were enthusiastic to see blood and gore, strode ahead, making deadly sounds and raising heroic slogans. Khara observed evil portents as he started out for battle. Rama on the other hand witnessed auspicious omens. He ensured Sita's safety before he engaged in duel with Khara. He asked Lakshmana to escort her to a safer place.

As the clash between the titans ensued, heavenly beings assembled in space to watch the scene with bated breath. They wondered how Rama would single-handedly tackle the demons.

Khara's men continuously bombarded arrows and darts at Rama. The prince defended them skillfully and killed most of the demons including Dooshana. When the battle raged fiercely, Rama used the divine bow given to him by Sage Agasthya. He broke Khara's chariot with it. As Khara hurled his mace at Rama, the prince shattered it with his arrows. Soon Khara fell dead on the battlefield like the rest of his army.

"Hail Rama! Hail the son of Dasharatha! He has killed the rakshasas and restored peace in Dandaka," shouted the Devas, showering flowers on Rama.

Akampana reports to Ravana

Akampana, a demon who survived the battle, hurried to Lanka to report the debacle to Ravana. In the same breath in which he detailed the death of Khara, Dooshana, and their men, he extolled the indomitable might of Rama. Ravana bellowed when he heard Akampana praise Rama's skills and strength in such glowing terms. "I will show that mere mortal, my supreme power. Akampana, you will then know who is invincible."

"Oh, lord of Lanka, you underestimate Rama's power. When he is incensed by anger, he can cause floods, pick up the submerging earth, and cause the wind to cease. You cannot conquer Rama in battle or destroy him in any manner. But I do have an idea. Carry off his wife Sita, whose beauty defies all description. Without Sita, the love of his life, Rama will not survive.

Akampana's idea appealed to Ravana and he immediately took off on his aerial chariot to Panchavati. On the way he stopped to meet his maternal uncle Mareecha and seek his help in accomplishing his mission. He updated Mareecha on the fall of Janasthana and the death of Khara and his entire army. Ravana then conveyed to Mareecha that he would avenge the death of his brother by whisking Sita away and thereby cause Rama's demise. On hearing Ravana's plan, Mareecha advised him against the plot, saying that such an act would certainly bring about his own destruction.

"Whoever counseled you to commit this vile deed is either misguided, or he does not have your wellbeing at heart. Be satisfied with keeping your wives happy and enjoying life with them. Leave Rama and his wife alone," Mareecha advised.

Soorpanaka seeks revenge

Ravana heeded Mareecha's counsel and abandoned the idea of abducting Sita. When he returned to Lanka, Soorpanaka rushed into his chamber with the ferocity of a tornado, causing those present, to tremble in fear. Her thirst for revenge against Rama escalated to monumental levels with the death of Khara. She now sought Ravana's intervention to crush Rama. She recounted to her brother how Rama and Lakshmana had insulted her and disfigured her.

"How can you sit here in peace when your land is threatened by two petty creatures from the mortal world?"

Soorpanaka hollered at Ravana. "Avenge my defacement. Punish Rama for having slayed our brother Khara. Carry away that lovely Sita and make her your wife." Soorpanaka cleverly manipulated Ravana and instigated him to achieve her own ends.

Ravana could no longer contain his desire to possess Sita when he heard his sister describe her beauty in glowing terms. Once again he fell prey to imprudent advice. He succumbed to the temptation of abducting Sita. For a second time he approached Mareecha to help him kidnap Sita.

Mareecha, who was fully aware of Rama's supreme power, appealed to Ravana to desist from the dishonourable act. "In committing this unholy crime of coveting another man's wife, you will gain nothing except death and damnation. Do not be the cause of your own downfall and that of your kingdom." Mareecha enumerated the innumerable qualities of Rama whose power and prowess, he emphasized, were fathomless. "By indulging in this sinful act, you are playing with fire. Rama's rage is bound to scorch you to ashes."

As if to lend credibility to his counsel, Mareecha recounted to Ravana his own experience of facing Rama. "When he was a mere lad, Rama bound me and threw me into the ocean when I tried to ruin a sacrifice that the great sage Vishwamitra was performing. On yet another occasion I escaped being killed by Rama when I was roaming the Dandaka forests in the guise of a large stag. When I saw him in Dandaka, I charged at him to kill him, seeking revenge for my defeat at his hands, years ago. By dint of my cunningness, I slipped away before I could be hit by his most powerful arrows. But the two ogre friends who accompanied me on that occasion were killed by Rama's arrows. Since I have escaped death at his hands twice earlier, I no longer wish to confront him."

The golden deer

Ravana, however, remained adamant in pursuing his objective. Mareecha reluctantly gave in to his nephew's whims. Ravana, meanwhile, had his plans well laid out, to the last detail, for Mareecha to follow.

Ravana and Mareecha flew in the former's golden chariot and reached Panchavati. Once there, they executed their plan. Mareecha turned himself into a wonderful golden deer and set off to draw Sita's attention.

The deer romped and gamboled around the dense trees surrounding Rama's ashram. The silver spots on his golden body shone like twinkling stars. Sita was gathering flowers in the forest when she spotted the magical deer. She was bewitched by the dazzling splendour of this creature scampering before her.

She called out to Rama and Lakshmana, "Come out and see this magnificent deer! What colour, what mischievous eyes it has. Look how playful it is. Bring it for me. We will rear it as our pet," she begged of Rama.

The ever alert Lakshmana suspected the deer to be a rakshasa in disguise, perhaps Mareecha who was known for assuming this form. He observed, "Has anyone ever heard of, or seen a real deer with such fancy looks, glittering in gold, silver and precious stones!"

But Sita was so fascinated by the creature that she insisted on Rama fetching it for her. She expressed her desire to have the lovely golden skin of the deer if Rama was unable to bring the creature, alive to her. Rama who did not want to disappoint Sita, gave strict instructions to Lakshmana, not to leave her alone even for a moment while he went after the deer. The spotted creature frisked and frolicked, moving deeper into the jungle, far away from their ashram. Rama followed. When Rama grew tired of the chase, he shot an arrow at it. It pierced its heart and the creature collapsed.

However, before falling down dead, Mareecha assumed his real form. As planned, he shouted, "Ah Sita, ah Lakshmana," imitating Rama's voice. Rama recalled Lakshmana's astute observation about the deer being Mareecha in disguise when he heard the dying creature call out to Sita and Lakshmana in his voice. Fear gripped Rama. He was sure Sita would be agitated on hearing Mareecha's words in Rama's voice. He began to run towards their ashram.

At the ashram, as soon as Sita heard Rama's cry of distress, she panicked. She implored Lakshmana to go after his brother and rescue him from the danger that she thought he was in. Since Lakshmana had promised Rama that he would not leave Sita unguarded, he refused to budge. He comforted Sita by telling her that Rama who was unassailable, would come to no harm. But Sita who was gripped by fear, lost all reason. She refused to be pacified. Instead, she accused Lakshmana of having evil designs on her. She charged him of being a wolf in sheep's guise, an enemy of Rama who feigned brotherly love for him. "Because of your greed to get me, you would allow Rama to die. Don't you ever be deluded that I would even look at any man other than my Rama."

Sita's words pierced Lakshmana's heart. Sita who was extremely agitated, continued her invective against her brother-in-law and threatened dire consequences if he refused to go after Rama and save him.

Lakshmana was no longer able to bear Sita's barbed remarks. He was also fearful of her threats of ending her life if he refused to seek out Rama and help him. He left her unguarded, and went in search of Rama. An uneasy feeling niggled him as he left their hermitage. Lakshmana had a nasty premonition that he may not see Sita upon his return with Rama.

Ravana in saffron robe

Ravana who had hid himself amidst the thick bushes watched the altercations between Sita and Lakshmana. As soon as he saw Lakshmana depart, leaving Sita alone, he executed his plan. Ravana attired himself in a saffron robe, and wore a garland of rudraksha around his neck. He disguised himself as an ascetic, and with staff and kamandala in hand, he approached Sita, chanting mantras.

Sita most respectfully, offered him fruits. After making some idle conversation with her, Ravana made his real intentions known to her.

"I have come to take you as my wife," he said. "Come, let us go to my kingdom, Lanka."

Sita was shocked at his daring behaviour. She derided him with angry words. Ravana turned a deaf ear. Instead, he boasted of being unmatched in might and skills by anyone else in all the three worlds. Ravana who was infatuated with passion to possess her, grabbed Sita and set her on the chariot which then began to rise in the air. Sita cried out to Rama and Lakshmana for help.

"Oh my lord, where are you? Here is this wicked rakshasa who has evil designs on me. Help, help! Oh faithful brother, Lakshmana, rescue me from this demon!"

As Ravana's aerial car rose higher and higher, Sita cried out to all of nature to help her. She called out to the trees and creatures of the Dandaka forest to inform Rama of the grave danger in which she was placed.

Jatayu fights Ravana

Just as the aerial car gained height Sita noticed old Jatayu perched on a tree top. She called out to him, asking him for help. Jatayu who had been asleep, woke up with her wails. He realized that she was in trouble when she called out the names of Rama and Lakshmana. Soon he spotted Ravana whisk her away in his vehicle. He immediately flew in front of the car and blocked its path.

"Oh learned king, you are a protector of people. It is your duty to honour and protect all women. Are you not committing a grave sin by carrying Sita away?"

When Jatayu realized that Ravana was in no mood to relent, he challenged him to a fight. "I am old and have no weapons to fight you. Yet I cannot stand by and watch you take Sita away. If you are not a coward, get off your chariot and face me!"

A clash between the two giants began. Ravana hurled deadly darts at Jatayu. The eagle king tore Ravana's flesh with his talons. He broke the demon's chariot into several pieces and killed the mules harnessed to it. He fought like a true hero, but Ravana was too strong for the ageing warrior bird. He chopped off Jataayu's wings and claws. The bird fell to the ground, grievously wounded.

Sita who looked upon Jatayu as a father, cried in anguish at his plight.

"Great king indeed, you are! How valiant you are, to steal another man's wife in his absence! How courageous you are, to strike an old and unarmed bird! The world will certainly remember you for these shameful deeds!"

Sita turned crimson with rage and volleyed these scornful words at Ravana.

But the ten-headed king of ogres was unperturbed. He tightened his grip on her and soared in the air. He proceeded towards Lanka, flying over mountains and rivers. As Sita looked down she observed a group of vanaras sitting on a mountain peak. With quick presence of mind, she removed her sash and bundled some of her ornaments in it. She flung the package down hoping to draw the attention of the vanaras with it. She expected them to pick up the bundle and turn it over to Rama when he came looking for her. She believed it would serve as a clue to indicate the direction in which she was taken.

As the chariot rode on in the sky, the Sun hid behind the horizon. The earth was plunged in darkness.

Sita in Lanka

"This is Sita. Serve her as you would serve me," Ravana ordered the rakshasis as soon as he reached Lanka and entrusted her to the care of the rakshasis. He then summoned eight of the most powerful ogres of Lanka and asked them to spy over Rama in Janasthana. The ogres assumed invisible forms and settled down in Janasthana to discharge the task given to them.

Sita was in tears, overwhelmed with grief. "My lord, I firmly believe you will soon come to save me. It is this belief that consoles me and makes me feel bold to face this demon," she said to herself.

Ravana tried to entice Sita with all the gold, jewels and wealth in Lanka. Sita was unmoved and she fearlessly challenged Ravana. She placed a blade of grass between herself and Ravana while talking to him. "Do not entertain hopes of winning me. It is only a matter of time before

Rama comes here to rescue me. You cannot escape the ruin you have brought upon yourself by committing this evil act."

Sita's unyielding words infuriated Ravana. "I give you twelve months to decide your fate. Make your choice; either you willingly become my wife, or be prepared to get cooked as meat for my breakfast", he warned Sita.

He then turned to the rakshasis attending on Sita and ordered, "Leave her in Ashoka Vana. Break her pride and stubbornness. Make her see sense to accept me as her husband."

Ashoka Vana was a breathtaking garden attached to the women's apartments in Ravana's palace. It was verdant with trees, flowers and ornamental plants. Deer and peacocks romped freely in the garden. The park had some of the most exotic and colourful birds in the world. The avenues of green trees led to a huge lake with turquoise blue waters. The lagoon rippled with plops made by multicoloured fishes swimming in its glassy waters.

Water lilies and lotuses blanketed the ponds in Ashoka Vana. Ducks and swans swam gracefully in them, enjoying the warm glow of the sun. Nature's vibrant hues lifted Sita's spirits. They appeared to reinforce her faith that her Rama would soon save her from the clutches of evil Ravana.

At the same time that Sita was placed under the care of the rakshasis at Lanka, Brahma solicited Indra to visit her in Lanka. Since Sita refused any nourishment from the hands of the demon clan, he asked Indra to offer her a meal of milk, rice and sugar – food most appropriately offered to the sacred fire. Nidra the god of sleep accompanied Indra to Lanka in order to put the demons to deep slumber while Indra met and spoke to Sita.

"I am Indra, come here at Brahma's behest, to offer you food fit to be served as an oblation to the holy fire. Oh princess of Videha, do not starve from grief for having been placed in this land of demons. Kindly partake of this offering which will nourish and sustain you for years to come," Indra pleaded with Sita when he met her in Ashoka Vana.

Sita, who was wary of being deceived by the ogres time and again, and who was also familiar with the unique symbols and emblems associated with various gods, asked Indra to prove his identity. Indra did as asked. Sita was convinced of Indra's identity. She paid respects to him as she would, her father. She then gladly accepted the offering made by him.

Rama goes in search of Sita

Meanwhile, at Dandaka, Rama and Lakshmana realized that Mareecha in the guise of a golden deer, had tricked them. They rushed to their ashram, fearing for Sita. They were alarmed and upset to find her missing. They searched for her everywhere – amidst the dense forests, hills, mountains and river banks surrounding their abode.

Rama wept in grief. He kept repeating, "What I feared has happened! I am sure the rakshasas have made meat of her! You should not have left Sita alone, Lakshmana."

Rama rushed in and out of their hut, looking for Sita in every nook and corner. He frantically ran here and there like a man possessed, asking the trees, the shrubs, the streams, the hills and creatures of the forest, if they had seen his beloved Sita. Fear swelled by the minute when he found no signs of Sita. Tormented by grief, he broke down in uncontrollable sobs. He threatened to dry up the rivers, render birds wingless and incapable of flight, annihilate the world and wipe out the demon race from it.

Lakshmana felt pained on seeing Rama so distraught. He tried to console and comfort him. He reminded Rama of his innately composed nature and remarked that he was allowing sorrow and anger to cloud his thinking. For a short while, Lakshmana's composure seemed to act as ballast to Rama's unstable sensibilities. Rama seesawed between hope and despair, going through a roller coaster of contrasting emotions.

Lakshmana sought to awaken the sleeping stoic in Rama and inspire him with courage. "Misery is but a passing cloud and who, born in this world is free from it? Rama, we are mere mortals. Even the likes of Indra, Vasishta and Yayati have not been spared from sorrow. Even the gods and celestial beings cannot escape fate. No one, absolutely no one, is immune from pain. Take heart, dear brother and do not give way to depression. Let us seek out the fiend who has brought this misery upon us."

The brothers intensified their search for Sita in Janasthana. As they ventured deeper into the forest, they spotted scattered flowers and golden beads which Rama identified as belonging to Sita. They followed the trail and came upon a spot where they saw signs of a recent scuffle. Moving close, they observed blood stains, crushed armour, smashed fragments of a chariot, royal headgear, broken jewels and such other material. They then noticed Jatayu lying in a pool of blood. Initially Rama mistook the bird for a demon in disguise, one who had devoured Sita. He rushed forward to kill the bird. Jatayu then informed Rama of the misfortune that had befallen Sita. "Ravana, the King of Lanka has carried off your dear wife. I tried to stop him. I battled with him and broke his chariot. But he was too strong for me. He cut off my wings and legs. I am on the verge of death. My love for you has enabled me to hold on to my breath so that I could inform you of Sita's fate. Bless me Rama, so that I may die in peace."

Tears welled up in Rama's eyes as he embraced the dying bird. Dasharatha's son once again wallowed in self-pity. "I lost my kingdom, have been banished from my land, I lost my father and could not even perform duly his last rites. My wife has disappeared and I have no clue to her whereabouts, and now I have lost Jatayu, a loving ally who was like a father to me. Could anyone be more unlucky than I am?"

After performing Jatayu's last rites and laying him to rest, Rama and Lakshmana continued their search for Sita.

Kabanda directs Rama to Sugreeva

As they wandered into the deep bowels of the forest and wondered where to look for Sita, an ugly and gigantic form suddenly appeared before them. He was a demon with no head or feet. His mouth was on his pot-like belly and the only eye he had was located on his chest! He had two enormous hands with which he grabbed his victims.

He introduced himself to Rama and Lakshmana as Kabandha and immediately sprung into action. He seized the brothers, one with each hand. In a rare moment of weakness, Lakshmana lost his composure and was overcome with fear. He implored Rama to escape from the clutches of the monster by sacrificing him, and proceed in search of Sita. As Rama urged Lakshmana to keep his cool, Kabandha threatened to devour them. Thinking swiftly, Rama said to Lakshmana, "Let's cut off his hands."

No sooner had the brothers cut off the monster's arms, Kabandha spoke, "Rama, I paid the price for my evil deeds with this ugly form. Now, I am redeemed by your divine intervention." Kabandha then breathed his last and ascended heaven.

Kabandha who was born as a demon, was once a handsome lad. He was granted the boon of long life by Brahma. He became arrogant and assailed Indra on the battle field. Indra struck him with arrows in such a manner that Kabandha's thighs and face receded into his torso. Unable to bear this grotesque form, Kabandha begged Indra to kill him instead. Indra informed him that he would be freed from his sin when Rama and Lakshmana would sever his arms.

However, before Kabandha departed he asked Rama and Lakshmana to go to the banks of the Pampa River and meet Sugreeva. "Befriend him and he will help you to find Sita," Kabandha informed. Sugreeva was a vanara who, after being driven out of his kingdom by his brother Vaali, took refuge in Rishyamooka Hill.

Shabari

Rama and Lakshmana, acted upon Kabandha's suggestion and proceeded towards Pampa River. On the way they spotted an ashram. As they approached the hermitage, they heard someone calling out Rama's name.

She was Shabari, a disciple of Sage Mathanga. The sage had shed his mortal coils, but Shabari waited for the arrival of Rama as foretold by her guru. She had lost count of the days which passed into weeks, months and years as she patiently awaited Rama's arrival. It was his name that she had on her lips all the time. Every day she would gather fresh juicy fruits from the forest trees for her Rama who she was certain, would come any day, any time. Years rolled by. There was no sign of Rama. But Shabari did not give up hope. Her heart told her Rama would undoubtedly come, if not today, tomorrow. Countless 'tomorrows' had passed by and yet there was no sight of Rama. Shabari was firm in her belief and continued to wait for Rama, gathering fruits for him, every day.

That evening, as she stepped out of her hut calling out Rama's name, she saw two men approaching her. In an instant, she knew her Rama had come! She forgot her age and ran towards him calling out, "Rama, my Lord, Rama, Oh Rama." Rama gathered her in his arms and gently led her to the hut.

Rama and Lakshmana partook of the fruits Shabari lovingly offered.

"Rama, I held on to this mortal body all these years only to behold you. I'm blessed. Now that I've seen you with my eyes, I have fed you with my hands, I have no more desire left. Allow me to depart from this world." Those were the last words of that saintly woman.

Monkey friends

When they reached Pampa Lake, Rama became nostalgic. When he saw the lotus-ridden lake he was overcome by a rush of emotion and memory that was as intimate as it was compelling. He was reminded of Sita's enchantment when she had seen a similar waterbody at Panchavati.

Sugreeva was seized with fear when he saw Rama and Lakshmana approaching his hideout with weapons in hand.

"They are perhaps warriors sent by Vaali to kill me!" Sugreeva thought aloud. He immediately called Hanuman, his lieutenant. "Hanuman, find out who these two armed men are and what brings them here."

At Sugreeva's command, Hanuman approached Rama and Lakshmana, disguised as a mendicant. He prostrated before them and paid them due obeisance. His tone was soft and measured as he spoke to them with utmost reverence in chaste Sanskrit. He wished to know what brought the two sage-like, resplendent personages to Rishyamookha. "You have a regal look. Your rightful place is to rule. Yet you are wandering in the forest. You wear garments made of bark and have matted hair, like the ascetics in the forest land. Yet you are carrying bow and arrows like warriors. Who are you? Where have you come from? What has brought you to this part of the forest? This region stands honoured by your effulgent presence," he observed and bowed humbly before them.

Hanuman's face was aglow with intelligence and sensitivity as he spoke. Rama was highly impressed with the manner in which Hanuman made enquiries and delivered his message.

"Lakshmana, only someone who has mastered the Vedas and the science of grammar can speak with such clarity without blemish. Did you not notice his impeccable choice of words?"

Hanuman then revealed his true identity to them. "I am Hanuman, the son of Vayu, and a minister of Sugreeva, the glorious leader of monkeys. I come here as his emissary, seeking your friendship."

Rama was happy to learn Hanuman was Sugreeva's representative. "Lakshmana, I feel encouraged that the very Sugreeva whom we are looking for, is extending friendship to us."

Lakshmana narrated their story to Hanuman – their exile, their encounters with rakshasas and how the wily Ravana had stealthily carried away Sita. They were now roaming the forest, moving from place to place in search of Sita.

Hanuman was convinced that the brothers had nothing to do with Vaali. He carried them on his shoulders and flew to Sugreeva's hideout in the hills.

Friendship pact

A cordial relationship sprung up between the sons of Dasharatha and Sugreeva. Rama promised Sugreeva help in getting back his lost kingdom from Vaali. Sugreeva for his part, agreed to help Rama find Sita. The friendship between the siblings of Ayodhya, and Sugreeva was forged and formally solemnized, with fire as a witness.

When Sugreeva heard Rama speak of Sita's abduction by Ravana, he recalled that some of his companions had seen a rakshasa carrying away a woman who was shouting for help. In fact the woman in distress had dropped a bundle which the vanaras had collected. Rama was eager to see the package. Sugreeva had a vanara fetch it and handed it to Rama. Rama broke down and sobbed as he recognized Sita's sash which she had used to wrap up some items of jewelry worn by her. He felt so tortured by pain that it was left to Lakshmana to open the bunched up piece of cloth. Lakshmana recognized one piece of ornament as the anklet worn by Sita. Rama once again experienced the agonizing pangs of separation from his beloved. He kept turning over the jewels again and again, clasping them close to his chest. He rambled on, expressing his intense longing to see Sita. Rama was ridden with grief and his voice trailed off into vacant nothingness. Those around him could sense the pessimism that was seeping into him.

Sugreeva consoled Rama, saying "I too am separated from my wife for no fault of mine. Yet I do not lose hope. I am awaiting the opportune moment to get back whatever I have lost. Pious Rama, you are a shining example of courage, valour, virtue and righteousness. How can you give way to grief and abandon fortitude? If we allow ourselves to be mentally weakened by adversities, how are we to overcome them? I humbly request you, not to become overwhelmed by sorrow. In honour of the friendship I have avowed, I will help you find Mother Sita."

The vanara chief assured Rama that his huge army would find Sita. Rama felt comforted.

Lakshmana who was excited on seeing the ornaments, questioned the monkeys. He learned from them that the aerial car used by the rakshasa had headed south. "Now we know where to look for Sita," he said.

Brothers turned foes

"Vaali and I doted on each other and lived happily in Kishkinda, our kingdom, of which he was king. But one day fate intervened and we parted ways. We brothers became sworn enemies and continue to be so," Sugreeva began to narrate to Rama, his own story.

One day, a rakshasa named Maayaavi challenged Vaali to an instant fight. Vaali who never refused a combat, rushed out at Maayaavi. Sugreeva followed his brother. Seeing the siblings chase him, the demon ran faster and disappeared into a big cave.

Vaali, before going after Mayavi into the cave, took a vow from Sugreeva. "Promise me, brother, that you will stand guard at the cave entrance until I return after killing the demon."

"I promise, brother," replied Sugreeva. He waited long but neither Vaali, nor Mayaavi came out of the cave. However, Sugreeva soon heard ear-piercing cries emerge from the cave. As he stood pondering over what might have happened inside, he saw blood gushing out of the cave.

Sugreeva froze. His mind stopped working. He jumped to the conclusion that his dear brother had been killed by Mayavi. He did not want his brother's killer to escape after committing the heinous crime. He therefore blocked the cave entrance with a huge boulder and returned to Kishkinda. Thereupon he announced Vaali's death at the hands of the rakshasa.

Kishkinda was in chaos without a ruler. "Without a ruler, there will be no safety or security for anyone in our kingdom. For the good of our people, you must take on the responsibility of kingship and occupy the throne," Vaali's ministers pleaded with Sugreeva. Sugreeva assumed the throne of Kishkinda after all the ministers convinced him with their arguments.

But destiny had other plans. It was Maayaavi who had been slain by Vaali. The vanara hero Vaali was dismayed to find the cave blocked with a huge rock when he made to come out of it. Vaali, with much effort and difficulty dislodged the boulder and came out. He was blind with anger at Sugreeva who he believed had deliberately shut him up in the cave. When he reached his capital, his anger amplified when he saw Sugreeva sitting on his throne. "How wicked and cruel could you be? You deliberately shut me inside the cave for Mayaavi to kill me so that you could become king of Kishkinda!"

Sugreeva could not prove his innocence in the face of Vaali's uncontrolled wrath. Vaali banished Sugreeva from his kingdom.

However, some of the vanaras who were faithful to Sugreeva, accompanied him to Rishyamooka Hill. The hill was a safe haven for Sugreeva because Vaali would not access it. Vaali had been cursed by rishi Mathanga that he would die if he entered Rishyamooka.

"So here I am, Rama, living like a fugitive, having lost my kingdom, wife, and all else."

"Rest assured, I will kill Vaali and restore your kingdom to you," Rama promised Sugreeva.

Sugreeva was happy to have found an ally in Rama. Yet, he had a nagging doubt regarding Rama's ability to vanquish Vaali who was a powerful warrior. He wished to ascertain Rama's abilities. Sugreeva therefore related an incident to Rama, to impress upon him, Vaali's might. Dundubhi, the demon buffalo, endowed with the strength of a thousand elephants, once challenged Vaali to a duel. In the clash that followed, Vaali easily defeated him. With a single swift movement of his hand, he hurled the blood soaked body of the demon to a great distance. Unfortunately, the blood spilled by the side of sage Mathanga's hermitage. Enraged at this, Mathanga uttered a curse: "Whoever has committed this gruesome deed and thereby polluted my ashram and its precincts, will meet his end upon stepping into Rishyamooka!"

Sugreeva concluded his narration to Rama saying, "This is the reason I am safe at Rishyamookha. Vaali will not dare to take one step in this direction for fear of dying. You will now have an idea of how strong he is."

Rama proves his mettle

Rama wished to allay Sugreeva's fears and dispel his doubts. He informed Sugreeva that he was willing to accept any challenge set by him to prove that he was a good match for his brother Vaali. Sugreeva replied, "I wish to see you split just one of the seven giant sal trees here, with a single shot of your arrow. I would also feel comforted if you would lift with a single foot, the bones of Dundubhi that lie here in a heap, and fling it a great distance."

Sugreeva added, "It is not my intent to test you or belittle you. While I am fully aware of my brother's skills and strength, I have not seen your power. Hence I fear the havoc Vaali can create!"

To put Sugreeva's mind at rest, Rama lifted Dundubhi's bones with a single toe and flung them a distance, several times farther than what Sugreeva had asked for. But Sugreeva remained skeptical. When Vaali threw Dundubhi's carcass, it was weighty with blood and flesh. But now, the bones, free of moisture and flesh, were lighter and hence easier to throw.

Rama gave the ultimate proof of his potent power by splitting with his arrow, not one, but all the seven sal trees in a row, with a single shot.

Rama kills Vaali

Sugreeva felt at ease after he watched Rama display such supreme strength. He was now ready to challenge Vaali to a duel. The plan was for Rama to hide behind a tree and strike Vaali when the brothers fought each other. A fierce battle ensued between the siblings who strikingly resembled one another. Rama was unable to distinguish Vaali from Sugreeva. He did not wish to risk killing Sugreeva in the bargain. Sugreeva was unable to defend Vaali's onslaught. He speedily beat a retreat to his refuge, Rishyamookha.

Rama once again asked Sugreeva to fight Vaali. This time, Lakshmana gave Sugreeva a garland to wear around his neck to differentiate him from his brother. Vaali's wife Tara was apprehensive about her husband's confrontation with Sugreeva and pleaded with him to refrain from accepting the challenge. "By the manner in which he dares you, I fear this will be no mean combat. I am sure he has allies who can harm you." Tara informed Vaali of the alliance that Sugreeva had forged with the sons of Dasharatha. She advised her husband to end the hostility with his brother for the wellbeing of everyone. Vaali refused to heed Tara, saying he would fight Sugreeva under all circumstances.

As the brothers fought each other, Rama struck Vaali at the opportune moment and mortally wounded him. While life still lingered feebly in the fallen Vaali, he reproached Rama for not facing him directly in battle. "You have belied your virtuous and noble birth by indulging in a sinful act. You have killed me, a monkey who did not harm you or your territory in any way," Vaali said to Rama as he lay dying.

Rama justified his action by telling Vaali that he had only received the punishment that was due him.

Both Vaali and Sugreeva repented their rash deeds as Vaali counted the minutes before life ebbed out of him.

Before he breathed his last, Vaali entrusted Sugreeva with a responsibility: "Kishkinda is now yours to rule. You must be a father to my son Angada and take good care of him, and take Tara as your wife."

Sugreeva, Angada and Tara felt profound sorrow at Vaali's demise. Rama asked Sugreeva to conduct Vaali's last rites in a befitting manner. Sugreeva performed his brother's obsequies with the help of Angada and Tara.

Sugreeva crowned king

Once Vaali was laid to rest, Rama wished Sugreeva well and also reminded him to begin the search for Sita at the end of the rainy season. The Ikshvaku brothers then took leave of Hanuman, Sugreeva and the rest of the vanaras, to dwell in the caves of Mount Prasravana on the outskirts of Kishkinda.

Sugreeva marched to Kishkinda, joyful to return to his city. Amidst pomp and pageantry, he was crowned king and Angada, the prince regent.

The monsoons had abated and given way to autumn but Sugreeva was so overjoyed to regain his kingdom that he indulged in the pursuit of pleasures, unmindful of his promise to Rama.

Lakshmana's anger

Prasravana Mountains which Rama and Lakshmana had made their home, abounded with aromatic shrubs and trees and inhabited by several species of wild creatures. But Rama barely enjoyed his environs for he fretted over Sita's wellbeing, and longed to have her with him. He constantly thought of her and the predicament she would be facing at the hands of Ravana. He grew restless as the rains had stopped and yet there was no sign of Sugreeva gearing up for action to look for Sita. He felt deep anguish and expressed to Lakshmana, his misgivings at Sugreeva's indifference in keeping his word.

"Lakshmana, now that the monsoons have abated, it is time for kings to carry out conquests and undertake expansion of their kingdoms. But I see no signs of Sugreeva making any effort to look for Sita. It appears as if he has forgotten my goodwill gesture. He shows no gratitude for the service I rendered him."

Laskhmana was angry that Sugreeva had caused Rama such distress. He was beside himself with rage. He entered Kishkinda, bow in hand, to demand an explanation from Sugreeva for his apparent apathy. He was even willing to fight and destroy Sugreeva if the need arose. The vanaras who saw Lakshmana seething with anger, fled from his approach. The leader of the monkeys rushed to Sugreeva to communicate to him, Lakshmana's arrival.

Meanwhile Hanuman who perceived Sugreeva's pursuit of luxury to intoxicating levels, gently reminded him of the task before him. The mighty son of Vayu told Sugreeva, "The spirit of friendship must be honoured and adhered to. As Rama's friend, and as an upright and respectable king, it is only appropriate that you uphold your honour and dignity by delivering your pledge to Rama. You must begin your search for Sita."

Sugreeva acknowledged the just and wise words of Hanuman. He gave orders for the vanara forces stationed at various points in Kishkinda, to assemble before him. He said, "no matter what I do in return, it will be insignificant in comparison to what he has done for me. I regret that I have inadvertently caused Rama and you pain by indulging in my own enjoyment, unmindful of my promise to Rama. Please inform Rama that I earnestly beg his pardon. I shall immediately press my vanara force into action to look for Mother Sita."

Lakshmana was now satisfied that Sugreeva would take his promise to Rama seriously and begin the search for Sita. He returned to convey to Rama, the vanara king's message to him. "Brother, Sugreeva has assured me that he would send his vanara sena in all four directions to look for Sita," Lakshmana reported to Rama.

Sugreeva's army sets out to find Sita

Meanwhile the vast monkey army assembled. It contained stalwarts like Angada, Hanuman, Jambavan and several others. Sugreeva made four divisions of his army. He sent one division each to the East, West, North and South, to look for Sita. He gave orders to the leaders of each battalion before they left on their mission, "Sita must be discovered. You must bring news of her within a month."

The brigade led by Angada which went south consisted of Hanuman and Jambavan the bear, among others. Sugreeva vested Hanuman with special responsibility, saying, "Son of Vayu, you possess the strength and intelligence of your father. You alone can successfully accomplish this task. Make haste and find Sita."

Rama gave Hanuman his signet ring, saying, "When you find Sita, give her this ring. She will be comforted that you are my messenger."

Hanuman saluted his king Sugreeva, and Rama, before taking leave of them. He headed South with his army.

Each contingent of Sugreeva's army was sincere in wanting to unite Rama with Sita. They began their search for Sita enthusiastically, heading in the direction they had been allotted.

The vanaras spread like ants in all directions looking for Sita. They crossed rivers, leaped upon mountains and combed every inch of the forests for her. Sugreeva's forces that had gone in the East, West and North directions, returned at the end of the month, unsuccessful in their attempt.

Hanuman and his team searched the forests and caves of the mountains, but did not get a single clue to Sita's whereabouts. They pressed forward and arrived at a vast desert. The monkeys felt their energy sapped by the scorching heat of the sandy terrain. The simians were thirsty, hungry, weak and tired, and became desperate when they did not see any vegetation or water. They feared that they would perish and were overwhelmed with sadness and despair in not succeeding in their mission of finding Sita.

Their sagging spirits rose when they suddenly experienced a gust of chill breeze. As they turned to take in lungsful of the whiff that caressed their face, they noticed a group of birds flying out of a hole, not far away. The monkeys became curious and rushed to the place from where the birds flew out. They felt they had found a passage which would take them to a cool region blessed with water. They were so desperate to escape the heat of the forest and get some water to drink, that they ventured to explore by going down the hole in single file. As they proceeded, it became darker and darker, so much so that they could barely see the vanara just ahead of them. Desperation turned to fear. The monkeys panicked, thinking that they were trapped in an unknown dungeon. Just then, a ray of light streaked through the dungeon and gave them cause for cheer. The passageway became wider and soon they saw a sprawling carpet of lush grass spread before them. They were astonished to see a beautifully laid out city with mansions, streets, gardens and fountains. As they rushed towards the water front, an elderly monkey stopped them when he saw a woman ascetic seated on a deer skin. When the monkeys approached her, the kind looking hermit slowly opened her eyes.

Hanuman told her that they served Sugreeva, the Lord of Kishkinda and were on a mission to find Sita, Rama's wife. The gentle lady, whose name was Svayamprabha, could see that the vanaras were famished. She asked them to help themselves to fruits from the orchard, without causing damage to the trees, and quench their thirst with water from the stream.

When the monkeys' hunger was sated and they were sufficiently invigorated, they resumed their search. But they were dismayed when they could not find an exit. Hanuman again approached Svayamprabha for help.

She told Hanuman that they were in a city that was built underground by Maya the asura architect. He had constructed it for his daughter Hema who was away, visiting Devaloka. "Hema has left the place in my charge. Maya has designed the place in such a way that no one who dares to enter it can escape from here," Swayamprabha revealed.

However, she assured Hanuman that she would help them to get out of the place with her yogic power. The monkeys closed their eyes tight upon Svayamprabha's request. They were thrilled and amazed to find themselves on the shore of the southern sea when they opened their eyes.

Sampati

"We have come to the very end of the land and nowhere did we see Mother Sita," brooded Angada.

"We are nearing the deadline set for us to find Sita."

"How can we get back to Kishkinda after failing to find Sita."

"How can we face Sugreeva and Rama?" Each of the vanaras lamented in his own way, reflecting upon their failure to locate Sita.

An old vulture perched on a tree atop a cliff was listening to the vanaras, unnoticed by them.

"It looks like Jatayu lost his life in vain when he fought to save Sita from Ravana," joined in another vanara.

At the mention of Jatayu's name, the old vulture became alert. He was none other than Sampati, Jatayu's brother.

He immediately approached the monkeys. "How do you know my dear brother Jatayu? You say he is no more! What happened to him? How did he die?" asked the old bird.

Sampati and Jatayu were the sons of Aruna, the god of Dawn. When they were children, they would compete with one another to see who could fly higher in the sky. On one such occasion, when Jatayu got quite close to the sun, the heat threatened to burn him. Sampati immediately spread his wings and protected Jatayu. Sampati's wings got burnt in the process and he fell on a hill, no longer able to fly, and ever since, began to live there.

The vanaras recounted to Sampati, how Rama, Lakshmana and Sita came to live in the forest. They told him of Jatayu's heroic efforts to save Sita from Ravana and of how he had lost his life in this attempt.

Sampati was saddened to hear of his brother's demise. He did not want Jatayu's efforts to go waste. He was determined to help the vanaras in whatever way he could. Though Sampati was old and weak, he had very sharp eyesight. He could see things that were very far away. He directed his gaze across the southern sea. Beyond the sea was the island of Lanka. There he spotted a woman sitting under an Ashoka tree, surrounded by rakshasa women. He informed the vanara team that Sita was held captive in Lanka, across the southern ocean, a hundred yojanas away.

Who could cross the ocean?

Now that they knew where to look for Sita, the monkeys wondered who among them was capable of making a leap across the southern ocean.

A vanara said he could cover ten yojanas with one leap. Another claimed he could cover fifty yojanas. Their commander Angada known for his strength said that he could possibly cover even a full hundred yojanas with one leap but was not sure whether he would have the strength to leap back to rejoin them.

Now there was silence. It became clear that no vanara could vault over to Lanka and come back with news of Sita.

"There is only one hero who can bound across to Lanka and also come back with information on Sita. It's him," said Jambavan, pointing to Hanuman who was sitting quietly, away from the other monkeys.

When Hanuman was a child, he tried to catch the sun thinking it was a juicy orange. Indra, the king of

Gods fearing that Hanuman would snatch the sun tried to stop him by throwing his thunderbolt at the young Hanuman. Hanuman's jaw broke when it was struck by Indra's powerful weapon, and he fell on the mountain, unconscious. Vayu became furious when he saw his son injured. He stopped his movements and became still. There was no air for anyone to breathe. All creatures became breathless and felt suffocated.

In unison, the gods begged Vayu to cast away his anger. But Vayu did not heed them. To pacify and appease him, Brahma and Indra granted several boons to Hanuman. "No weapon will be able to kill your son. He will be immortal," they assured Vayu. Thus mollified, Vayu resumed his function.

As a child, Hanuman was mischievous. Brahma's boons had made him so strong that none could control him. The sages who tired of his pranks, cast a spell on him saying that he would not remember his own power unless he was reminded of it by someone. "This is the reason why Hanuman is sitting there so quietly, oblivious of his own strength. But he alone is capable of crossing the ocean with a single leap over the vast water body," Jambavan explained to the vanaras.

He then approached Hanuman, accompanied by the rest of the vanara force.

"Hanuman, you alone can fulfill Sugreeva's promise to Rama. You can increase your size to whatever proportions you want. You can cross this sea in one single jump to reach Lanka," said Jambavan.

"Yes, Hanuman, you can cross the ocean in one leap," said Angada.

The vanaras raised a chorus, "Yes, Hanuman, You can. Hanuman you can, you can..."

Crossing over to Lanka

The vanaras surrounding Hanuman kept chanting, "Yes, Hanuman, you can cross the ocean in one leap, you can. Hanuman you can, you can ..."

As the chorus grew louder, Hanuman grew in size. When the animated shouts reached a crescendo, Hanuman stood tall, spanning the earth and sky.

He prayed to all the gods and paid obeisance to his father Vayu. He silently saluted his master, Rama. As he took a deep breath, flexed his muscles, and pressed his feet on the hill, the ground on which he stood trembled, and many trees got uprooted.

In one quick move, Hanuman lifted himself off the mountain peak and was soon air-borne, soaring far and high, speeding towards Lanka. The uprooted trees which were caught in the momentum of Hanuman's mighty heave, flew after him, as if they wanted to give him their company. Hanuman looked like an enormous comet on fire as he travelled in space.

Hanuman's huge form cast a shadow on the sea as he cruised across the sky, and appeared like a ship that was being tossed about by fierce winds and swelling waves. He looked like a winged mountain, dragging a trail of clouds behind him. The heavenly beings showered flowers upon him and blessed him, and wished him success. The merciful sun kept himself mellow and the Wind god fanned him with cool breeze.

When Hanuman was half way down to Lanka, a huge mountain rose up from the very depths of the ocean. The golden-hued mountain assumed a human form and stood on its own peak before Hanuman. "Oh noble Hanuman, I am Mount Mainaka. Since you are serving Rama, allow me to be useful to you. I would be greatly honoured if you would descend down on my peak and rest yourself awhile before continuing your journey." Mainaka spoke to Hanuman and offered him fruits and roots to reinvigorate himself for the long and arduous flight to Lanka.

The god of the ocean was indebted to King Sagara of the Ikshvaku dynasty. He therefore desired to help Hanuman find Sita, and approached Mount Mainaka to rise up from the ocean bed. "Mighty mountain, you are capable of growing in any direction. Please rise up from the waters and allow Hanuman to rest on you."

Mainaka who was obliged to Hanuman's father Vayu, recounted to Hanuman his own story. "We mountains once enjoyed flying because we had wings. Just like Garuda, we too could fly across the sky at enormous speed. But all living beings including the rishis, devas and gandharvas feared that we might fall upon them and cause them harm. In a fit of temper, Indra aimed his thunderbolt at our wings. I was fortunate to escape his fury because your father, the glorious Vayu, intercepted Indra's axe as it approached me, and saved me. He dropped me into the ocean with my wings intact." Mainaka narrated this incident to Hanuman and once again urged the vanara hero to partake of his hospitality.

Hanuman thanked Mainaka for his offer but politely declined, saying, "I have vowed to myself that I shall not rest until I accomplish my mission and find Sita.

Hanuman crosses the hurdles

Mainaka joined his hands in salutation to Hanuman who continued his journey towards Lanka with greater speed. The Devas, Rishis, Siddhas and Gandharvas wanted to test Hanuman's might. They set Surasa, the mother of serpents, to execute their plan. Surasa assumed the form of a hideous monster and blocked Hanuman's path. She opened her mouth wide and asked him to enter it. "Well, then open your mouth wide enough for me to enter," said Hanuman, growing to a humongous size. As soon as the demon widened her mouth, Hanuman shrunk himself to the size of a thumb. Even before Surasa realized it, Hanuman entered her mouth, and came out of it, unscathed.

Surasa assumed her true form when she realised how cleverly Hanuman had tricked her. She blessed him and wished him success in finding Sita.

Hanuman continued towards Lanka, braving lightning, thunderstorms and torrential rains. He appeared to be gloriously suspended in the sky, like a wingless bird, the size of a mountain. But his troubles were not yet over. An ogress of mammoth size by name Simhika, who saw his enormous form, said to herself, "This creature would make a good meal for me." She immediately grabbed Hanuman's shadow and tugged at it.

Hanuman suddenly felt his strength weaken. When he turned around to determine the cause of the obstruction, he noticed Simhika floating above the ocean. She was a demoness of great strength who could pull anyone simply by wrenching their shadow! When he recognized Simhika,

Hanuman swelled himself to look like a huge mass of rain clouds. Simhika then opened her mouth as wide as the distance between the sky and the nether world. Hanuman once again revealed his ingenuity. He reduced himself to a tiny form and jumped into the ogre's mouth. He came out of her mouth after ripping apart her insides with his claws. She fell into the ocean, dead.

Hanuman surmounted the various obstacles on his way to Lanka with quick witted intelligence. He reached Lanka without further delay. "I have to be alert now. I should look for Sita without drawing attention to myself," Hanuman cautioned himself and assumed his normal size.

Hanuman in Lanka

Hanuman perched himself on a tree on the outskirts of the city, to survey Lanka. Ravana's kingdom stood splendorous on Mount Trikuta, encircled by a gigantic fort wall. There were armed guards and soldiers everywhere in the fort city. Hanuman pondered, "The rakshasas can neither be won over by good words, nor be appeased with gifts. Diplomacy too will not work with them. How will the vanara army cross the mighty ocean? Only Angada, Neela, Sugreeva and I, can leap across this infinite water body... No, but first things first! Let me find out the whereabouts of Sita."

As Hanuman walked towards the fort gate, Lankasri, the guardian deity of the city confronted him in all ferocity. She glared at him and demanded to know his identity and the purpose of his visit.

"Lanka is well protected. There is no way you will be able to come in. If you care for your life, just disappear!" she thundered.

Hanuman remained calm and unperturbed. "Who are you and why are you blocking my entry into the city?" He questioned Lankasri.

"I am the deity of Lanka who protects the city. I will kill you if you try to make your way in," she said, in a menacing tone.

Hanuman ignored her threats. He told her that he was determined to have a tour of Lanka, to enjoy its magnificence.

Lankasri was infuriated by Hanuman's insistence and impudence. She gave him a powerful punch.

Hanuman considered it discourteous to hit a woman with all his might. He therefore clenched his left fist and hit her lightly. But it was enough to shatter Lankasri's limbs and she fell down with a thud. When she got up, she dusted herself and addressed Hanuman in a voice that trembled with fear: "You are indeed an extraordinary monkey, a hero of great power and intelligence. Now let me tell you a little truth about myself." The Goddess of Lanka then revealed to Hanuman the prophetic words of Brahma who had said that when a monkey would overcome her, it would spell doom for Ravana and his rakshasa clan. "I have now become aware that you are the monkey mentioned by Brahma. And with your arrival here, our bad time is imminent. Go ahead, enter Lanka and fulfill the purpose for which you are here."

Hanuman jumped over the wall and entered the city, placing first, his left foot on its soil. The mansions and skyscrapers of Lanka glittered with gold, gems, ivory inlay sculptures. Colour was everywhere in Ravana's kingdom – on its streets, its palaces, ponds, parks and forests. Lanka was pulsating with music, dance and merrymaking. While some of the rakshasas were chanting the Vedas, there were others who sang hymns praising Ravana.

The heroic vanara observed the inhabitants of the city in an intoxicated state. He saw the rakshasas in their many shades of emotions and intelligence. Hanuman's keen intellect and sharp eyes noticed how even the ugliest among the monsters had dressed with care. He saw the good and virtuous demons intermingling with the evil ones, and yet remaining chaste and untainted. Hanuman saw many beautiful ladies with sound sensibilities. But he saw no signs of Sita.

Hanuman anxiously searched every nook and corner of Lanka for Rama's beloved. He conducted a house-to-house search but found her nowhere. Then he saw Ravana's palace on the mountain top, dazzle under the moonlit night. It was surrounded by a huge moat that was filled with lotus flowers. Hanuman entered the palace courtyard. Every area of the fortress was heavily guarded with elephants, horses, chariots and aerial cars.

He finally approached Ravana's personal stronghold where the demon king resided. It was fortified by several gates. In décor it bore semblance to Kubera's mansion. The stately aerial vehicle, the Pushpaka Vimana, which itself had the appearance of a castle, graced the centre of the palace. It was held aloft by large white swans. It was built by the divine architect, Vishwakarma himself. The chariot of exceptional speed and splendor could travel at any height, unobstructed by anyone or anything, including the wind.

The Pushpaka Vimana originally belonged to Kubera, the god of wealth. Brahma had rewarded him with it for the austerities he had performed. It was entirely bedecked with gems. Ravana overpowered Kubera and acquired the heavenly car for himself.

Hanuman entered Ravana's palace after looking for Sita everywhere else. Fragrance from burning incense and aroma of cooking delicacies, wafted as Hanuman went in. He beheld beautiful women in deep slumber. The floral wreaths on their curly tresses and their ornaments lay scattered around them. Their garments were disheveled as they lay sprawled in undesirable postures. It was obvious to Hanuman that these women had drunk themselves to exhaustion.

There were several women here, who came from the virtuous homes of rishis, kings, gandharvas, devas and daityas. The daughters of these noble men were objects of Ravana's fancy. He had won most of them in battles.

Hanuman's attention was then drawn to a lavish bed of quartz. It was inlaid with gemstones, ivory and gold. On it he saw Ravana, handsome and resplendent in all finery, blissfully asleep. A few of his wives were lying asleep at his feet.

On another grandly decked couch, Hanuman saw a woman looking graceful in sleep. The suave beauty of this fair-complexioned lady embellished the very chamber in which Hanuman saw her. He thought she must be the pious Sita and felt overjoyed. His mirth, however, was short lived. Hanuman thought to himself, "She can't be the devout daughter of Janaka, the righteous daughter-in-law of Dasharatha, and the beloved of Rama. For how would Sita, parted from Rama, sleep so peacefully? Sita of noble disposition, suffering pain on being separated from her dear Rama, would neither touch a drop of water nor sport jewelry."

In fact it was Mandodari, the pious wife of Ravana, who Hanuman beheld.

Even after undertaking a thorough and extensive search in the inner chambers of the palace, Hanuman drew a blank. He did not sight Sita anywhere. He was saddened that his efforts had not yet borne fruit. On the other hand, he was plagued by guilt for having closely scrutinized women who were wives of other men. He felt he had transgressed moral codes in doing so. He battled with his conscience and finally consoled himself thinking, "It is only my deep yearning to restore Sita to beloved Rama that has made me look closely at the women here. I do not entertain any impure thoughts towards these ladies."

Faith and doubt pulled like strings around his throat. Hanuman became despondent and his mind gave way to negative thoughts. Could Sita have lost her life pining for Rama? Would that cruel Ravana have killed her for not yielding to him? Is it possible that Sita died of fear, looking at the grotesque rakshasas in Lanka? Perhaps, Sita did not reach Lanka at all! Ravana might have lost his grip on her as he flew across the mountains and oceans. And she might have fallen to her death! Or she might have got suffocated to death because of Ravana's firm clasp of her throat. Probably, she is still alive, imprisoned in some dungeon in Lanka? Hanuman's mind was churning with endless possibilities on what might have happened to Sita.

However, despair and depression soon gave way to renewed hope. Hanuman recovered his equanimity and resolved to continue his search for Sita. Just then his roving eyes spotted an area in Lanka he had not searched. It was the magnificent Ashoka Vana, surrounded by a high wall.

Hanuman in Ashoka Vana

Hanuman, without losing more time, shrunk himself to an almost invisible size and entered Ashoka Vana. He prayed to all the gods and Devas to help him succeed in his efforts. By now it was daybreak. Hanuman was spellbound by the heavenly park. Spring was in the air. Nature was at its bounteous best in the expansive garden.

Flowers were in full bloom. Ashoka Vana was paradise itself. Birds sang from their perch on trees. Peacocks, deer and other animals scampered freely in the vast expanse that was decked in gold, silver, gems and crystals. The mood in Ashoka Vana was chirpy as the rakshasas sang joyously and were engaged in playful activities.

Hanuman lost himself in the enchanting beauty of Lanka and its Ashoka Vana. He jumped on to a tree that was dense with branches and dark green leaves. From his post on this tree he explored Ashoka Vana, his eyes wandering around its every corner, looking for Sita.

Hanuman's eyes fell on a temple that towered tall in the Vana precincts. He then caught sight of a woman surrounded by demons as she reclined against a tree. Hanuman made himself even smaller and leaped on to the tree under which the lady sat.

He guessed her to be Sita. He had good reasons to suppose so. He saw on her the same earrings that Rama had described when he was leaving Kishkinda. The worn-out garment she wore, was of the same hue as the one she had thrown on Rishyamookha, with her jewels bundled in it.

She was thin and pale. She wore soiled clothes and little jewelry. Yet she shone like the moon. She looked sorrowful, yet serene. Surrounded by rakshasis she looked helpless yet not lacking in courage. He could hear her heartbeat. It was beating, Rama, Rama. Hanuman joined his hands and bowed his head. All of a sudden he exclaimed: "Behold! I have seen Mother Sita! I have seen Rama's beloved." The fears and misgivings that Hanuman had earlier experienced, melted in this newfound rapture of having discovered Sita.

Sita looked so divinely beautiful in complete contrast to the females sitting around her. Hanuman was charmed by her radiant look and admired her courageous demeanour in the face of adversity.

"How dignified and graceful she looks even when placed in this miserable plight," Hanuman thought to himself. He was eager to talk to her. He wanted to convey Rama's message to her. But he held his patience. He waited for darkness to fall and the rakshasis to sleep.

Hanuman's initial euphoria on discovering Sita, soon dissipated and gave way to distress. The princess of Mithila and consort of Rama, born into wealth, had seen neither want nor hardship. She, upon whom attendants waited, was now surrounded by demons of most ugly form, who were bullying her.

Though Hanuman carefully watched every movement in Ashoka Vana, his eyes remained focused on Sita. As twilight approached, he heard the chanting of Vedas followed by melodious strains from musical instruments. He soon saw Ravana walk towards Ashoka Vana, followed by his many demon wives.

Ravana cast amorous glances at Sita. To Sita, his smile imparted no warmth to his face; if anything, it made him look more threatening. He shamelessly professed his love for her, describing her beauty, feature by feature. "Don't imagine you will ever set eyes on Rama again! There is no way he will be able to get you back from me. Why do you pine for one who can offer you nothing but a life of an ascetic wandering in the forest? Marry me, and you will enjoy all pleasures of life. All my consorts will wait upon you. You can adorn yourself with an enormous variety of the most precious jewels you can ever hope to have."

Sita shuddered at Ravana's very sight. Though she sat under the tree in soiled clothes, her thoughts were unsullied. She could think of none other than her beloved Rama. Sita felt repulsed by Ravana's evil intents. She placed a blade of grass between herself and the demon king. As she wiped the tears that rolled down her cheeks, unchecked, she scoffed at Ravana's overtures and boldly confronted him: "Don't you dare compare yourself to my lord who is a fathomless well of goodness. Oh king of Lanka, stop seeking another man's wife; rest satisfied with your queens. If you wish to save yourself from destruction, seek Rama's forgiveness and friendship. He is ever-merciful and he will pardon you and protect you. There is none on this earth who can stand up to him. Did you not hear accounts of how he destroyed your brother Khara and hordes of other ogres in Janasthana, single-handed? Restore me to him and rescue yourself from falling down to greater depths of dishonour. Do not bring disaster upon yourself and your people."

Ravana's face contorted with rage on hearing Sita's sharp remarks. His eyes turned red, his nostrils flared, and his lips drew back from his teeth in a grating snarl. He kept his seething anger in control, and held his fists clasped by his sides. With teeth clenched, he threatened Sita, "You are lucky to get away with what you speak because of my love for you! Otherwise, you would be dead by now! It is high time you yield to my request. You have parried enough. I generously gave you twelve months' time of which only two months remain. Give me the good news soon."

Ravana's menacing tone made some of the noble ogres wince. They were daughters of gods and gandharvas who had been forcefully coveted by Ravana because he had won them in battles. They reassured Sita with subtle gestures and glances. Emboldened by their supportive gesticulations, Sita responded to Ravana's warning: "Oh ignoble creature, it certainly appears that Lanka does not have a single well-intentioned soul who can dissuade you from walking this evil path. Be assured that you will not escape punishment for this most immoral proposal that you have made to me, Rama's consort. Why, I myself have the power to reduce you to ashes this very moment! But I refrain from doing so because I have not sought my Lord, Rama's permission to do so. Wicked king of Lanka, become aware now, that I was not capable of being seized by you in the first place. What is happening, is destiny's drama to bring about your destruction!"

Ravana's anger increased with each word that Sita spoke. He shot back at her, I could kill you right away instead of pleading with you." The king of Lanka was unyielding. He wanted to possess Sita at any cost. He ordered the demons to bend and break Sita's spirits so that she would accede to his wish.

Ravana's most favourite wife, Mandodari, tried to calm him down and make him see reason. "Do you not realize that you will only bring misery upon yourself by craving for a woman who does not love you? Instead, you would be wise to love a woman who dotes on you." Ravana merely guffawed at Mandodari's logic as he departed from Ashoka Vana to his own palace.

The monstrous demons began to act upon Ravana's command. They cajoled, coaxed and bullied Sita to comply with his desire. "You should consider yourself fortunate to be the wife of one who has vanquished the mightiest of gods. What joy or comforts can Rama, driven out of his own kingdom, give you? Oh foolish woman, abandon your stubbornness and marry the powerful Ravana who adores you."

Sita felt repulsed by the sinful advice given by the ogres. "My Rama is my most prized jewel. What need have I for comforts when Rama is my consort? Whether he is a king or a wandering mendicant, I will remain devoted to him alone," Sita retorted.

Hanuman remained patient on his perch and heard every word of the conversations between Sita and Ravana and those between Sita and the other ogres. He realized in full measure, Sita's inherent dignity, her divine nature and her love for Rama.

Within moments, Hanuman also sensed that Sita was reaching breaking point as the ogres tortured and tormented her. Tears gushed down her cheeks and in despair, she wished herself dead. "Eat me if you will, but I will not heed your evil advice," she said. Sita was rendered incapable of reasoning as the rakshasa women continued to violently bash her emotionally. In sheer desperation, she cried out: "Oh Rama, Oh, Lakshmana, Mother Kausalya, will none of you come to my rescue! Rama, my life is meaningless without you. I don't see any signs of you coming to save me. I wonder what sin I committed in my previous birth to beget such sorrow now. It is only right that I put an end to myself and to the misery I experience!"

As Sita sat bewailing her lot, Trijata, an aged ogress who had hitherto been asleep, woke up with a jolt. Seeing Sita threatened by her co-ogresses, she warned them of the impending disaster that would befall them all. Trijata narrated to them, a dream she has seen which augured ill for their king and people. On the one hand, she had dreamt of Rama, Sita and Lakshmana with garlands around their necks, mount a celestial chariot drawn by several horses. On the other hand, she had a vision of Ravana, his siblings and sons, doused in oil, fall headlong from the backs of donkeys.

Meanwhile, Sita who was frustrated and depressed, decided to end her life by strangling herself with the cord she used for bundling up her hair. Just then, she observed auspicious signs on her body. Her left eye throbbed, her left arm palpitated and her left thigh pulsated. She felt the presence of Rama beside her. Sita was encouraged by these and other omens she considered as good. Her spirits lifted and with it, her mind cleared of the confusion she had earlier felt.

Hanuman meets Sita

It was the dark hours of the night and the rakshasis guarding Sita, tired from threatening her, fell into deep slumber. Hanuman was awaiting this opportune moment to approach Sita and convey Rama's message to her. However, his mind was riddled with questions. How should he approach Sita without startling her? How would he introduce himself to her? Once he identified himself, what would he tell her? Now that I have seen her and know her whereabouts, what if I depart from Lanka without meeting her? If I leave Lanka without reassuring her of Rama's arrival here to rescue her, she might give up her life! This would defeat the very purpose for which I have come here. But how do I initiate a conversation with the pious Sita? Well, I could talk to her in Sanskrit. But she might mistake me for Ravana in disguise! What if she cries out upon seeing me? The rakshasis would then wake up and seeing me, they would raise an alarm. Hanuman weighed the merits of the options before him. After much deliberation, he decided to remain hidden. He concluded that he would narrate Rama's story, from his birth, to the present, sitting on the treetop. He would include in this recital his own arrival at Lanka in search of Sita.

In soft tones, Hanuman began to sing the story and glory of Rama, beloved of Sita. He began extolling the virtues of King Dasharatha of the Ikshvaku family and then went on to recount the childhood and youth of his four sons. Hanuman related in a lucid manner, Rama's banishment from Ayodhya, his subsequent confrontations with several demons, of how he vanquished Khara in Janasthana and the consequent abduction of Sita. Hanuman completed his rendition by describing Rama's search for Sita in the forests of Dandaka. He sang the glory of the friendship that blossomed between Sugreeva, the vanara chief and Rama. He narrated how Rama had made Sugreeva the king of Kishkinda after killing his brother Vaali. Finally Hanuman melodiously sang, describing his own role as Sugreeva's chief minister who had now come to Lanka in search of Sita.

Hearing the story of Rama, Sita was delighted and scared at the same time. "Who could this be, who is singing beloved Rama's story in such soothing words? Perhaps, he is a rakshasa trying to trick me?"

Sita looked all around to locate the source of the voice. As she looked up, she saw a little monkey sitting on the branch above her. While she was wonderstruck on seeing him, she was also terrified at dreaming of a monkey. "Dreaming of a monkey does not auger well," Sita thought. "But sleep has eluded me ever since I was separated from Rama! No, this cannot be a dream!" she argued within herself. Sita thought the monkey's words were a figment of her imagination since she constantly thought of Rama. His name alone was eternally on her lips, mind and heart. She prayed to the gods that the monkey's words be true. As she turned over these thoughts in her mind and oscillated between hope and doubt, Hanuman gently came down from his perch. He stood before her, palms joined and head bowed in reverence to Sita. Hanuman was yet again struck by Sita, who was a picture of beauty, chastity, grace and poise.

He then spoke to her in a gentle voice, full of respect. "Oh, noble mother, may I know who you are and how you come to be here? From you demeanour and disposition, I gather you are the gracious Sita, consort of Rama, mercilessly carried away by the demon king of Lanka!"

Sita who was delighted to hear Rama's name, told Hanuman he was right in presuming she was Sita, Rama's wife. She then narrated her story to him.

Hanuman then introduced himself to her as Rama's emissary. He related to her the pangs of pain Rama suffered after losing her, and how he sought Sugreeva's help in finding her. Sita, however, was still doubtful of Hanuman's true identity. Hanuman sensed her hesitation. He immediately took out Rama's signet ring and handed it to Sita.

"Mother, Rama asked me to give this to you as proof that I am a messenger sent by him," said Hanuman, bowing respectfully before Sita.

Sita was overjoyed at this meeting with Hanuman. She took the ring from him and pressed it to her eyes repeatedly. It was as if she was seeing Rama himself.

"If Rama is grief-stricken as you say, why does he not come to rescue me at once? If Rama does not save me within two months, Ravana will make meat of me," Sita lamented. "Ravana is adamant on making me his wife. His youngest brother Vibheeshana, a virtuous soul, admonished him for having abducted me. He has repeatedly advised him to restore me to Rama. But Ravana remains stubborn. Vibheeshana's wife sent his daughter Kala to inform me of this. O noble Hanuman, ask Rama to come here and fetch me right away!"

Hanuman responded by telling Sita that Rama would be able to reach Lanka only after he, Hanuman himself returned to Kishkinda with news of his beloved Sita. "But mother, I myself can take you to Rama immediately. You may sit on my back as I leap across the ocean and take you to Mount Prasravana where Rama resides."

Sita was overjoyed by Hanuman's offer. Nevertheless, she declined it, saying: "It would be most worthy of Rama to take me back with him after he kills Ravana. So make haste and return with Rama to deliver me from this evil demon."

Hanuman comforted Sita: "Rest assured mother, Rama will surely save you from the wretched Ravana."

As Hanuman took leave of Sita, he asked her for a token to take back to Rama as proof of his having met her. Sita responded by telling Hanuman that a message to Rama was the best token she could give him. She narrated to Hanuman an incident that took place when they dwelt in a hermitage near the Mandakini River while serving their exile. A hungry crow that was greedy for meat repeatedly tried to peck Sita when she and Rama were relaxing. To Rama's amusement, Sita delicately defended herself by making mud balls and throwing it at the crow to shoo it away. The crow showed no signs of relenting. Sita who was exhausted from trying to ward off the crow, sought refuge in Rama's lap. While they were asleep in each others' arms, the crow returned to claw Sita's breasts. Blood from the wound, oozed on the sleeping Rama and he woke up. Rama was enraged with the crow's act. He pulled out a kusa grass from the garden and made it potent as the Brahmastra. As he made to strike the crow with it, the bird who was in reality Indra's son, begged Rama for forgiveness. However, the missile once discharged could not be recalled. Rama therefore spared the crow's life, but blinded its right eye with the weapon. When Sita finished recounting the incident to Hanuman, she questioned, "When Rama, my beloved, was so angered by a crow, that he immediately rose to fight it, why is he keeping quiet when Ravana has whisked me away with mal-intent?"

Sita then handed Hanuman a piece of her jewelry, saying: "Rama would be happy to see this as proof of your having met me. Give it to him when you reach Kishkinda."

Hanuman the destroyer

Hanuman desired to instill more confidence in Sita. At the same time he wanted to create fear in the minds of Ravana and his demons. He wanted to warn the demon king of his impending destruction at the hands of Rama.

After some deliberation, Hanuman once again assumed a mammoth form. He laid waste, the beautiful Ashoka Vana. He did this without destroying the area occupied by Sita in the Vana.

The sleeping rakshasis woke up, hearing the noises around them. They saw the huge monkey and the havoc he had created. They rushed to Ravana: "There is a huge monkey that has ruined our lovely AshokaVana. We also saw it talking to Sita."

Ravana was outraged when he heard this. "Kill this monstrous monkey," he shouted orders to his guards.

Hanuman was all set for the confrontation with Ravana's guards. He brandished his most cherished possession, his tail. He swished it around and leaped from one place to another. He attacked the soldiers and killed them all. When he was satisfied with the chaos he had created, he sat smugly on top of the pillared entrance gate of Lanka. He began singing praises of Rama and Lakshmana.

Hanuman shook the city of Lanka with loud roars that echoed throughout the region. The rakshasas trembled in fear at this. When Ravana was informed that his guards had been killed by Hanuman, he sent the mighty warrior Jambumali to capture the monkey. Soon messengers brought the news that Jambumali was killed in the battle with the monkey.

Ravana then summoned his favourite son Aksha and ordered him to fight Hanuman. Aksha, young and radiant with energy, rode on his golden chariot to battle Hanuman. When he saw the son of Vayu, he was impressed with the monkey's well-proportioned body.

Aksha said to himself: "This promises to be a well-poised battle. This monkey seems an enemy worthy of a fight." Aksha sent a volley of arrows at Hanuman. A fierce clash ensued between the two. As arrows rained on Hanuman, he skillfully avoided getting hit by them. He admired the courage and valour displayed by the youthful Aksha. As the battle progressed, Aksha grew mightier. Hanuman charged against his opponent's chariot and smashed it to pieces. The horses fell dead. Aksha was undaunted. He rose in the air, bow and arrow in hand. The battled raged fiercely in the air. Hanuman delivered the final blow and the young hero fell dead.

Ravana's wrath increased manifold when he heard Aksha had been killed. He called for his son Indrajit, the conqueror of Indra.

"None in the world can equal you in strength or foresight. You have mastery of all weapons. Your knowledge of battle tactics is unparalleled. Further, you have the coveted Brahmastra with you. Go, deal appropriately with this terrible monkey and return victorious," thundered Ravana.

Indrajit took Ravana's blessings and proceeded to meet Hanuman. The two combatants were equally matched in strength and skill. A powerful battle followed. All the celestial beings, the nagas, yakshas and siddhas gathered in the sky to watch this encounter. Darts and arrows flew in the skies. Hanuman rose in the sky becoming bigger than ever. He deftly fielded the weapons hurled at him. No matter how many arrows Indrajit showered on him, Hanuman stood strong.

"My arrows cannot destroy this monkey. My father was right. I can contain this creature only by using the Brahmastra," thought Indrajit to himself. The Brahmastra was the most powerful of weapons. Indrajit had received it from Brahma himself because of the austerities he had performed.

Without wasting time, Indrajit directed the Brahmastra at Hanuman. As soon as it touched him, Hanuman became helpless as he was bound by the weapon. He lay still and awaited the right moment to strike back.

The rakshasas gathered around him and began merry-making. They abused and shouted insults at him. They threatened to cut him to pieces.

"This monkey is not one to give up easily. He is perhaps, pretending to lie helpless. He might rise up suddenly and attack us." Some of the rakshasas began talking amongst themselves.

"Let us take no chances with him. Let us tie him with ropes," they concurred. Hanuman was duly bound tightly with ropes of jute and coconut fibre. He was then dragged through the streets of Lanka and taken to Ravana's court.

Hanuman surveyed his surrounds as he stood before the demon king. Ravana, clad in golden-coloured silken robes looked resplendent on his throne. The crown on his head glittered with gold and inlaid gems. Hanuman gazed at the rich ornamentation of his court, and at Ravana himself.

Hanuman had mixed feelings when he beheld Ravana in all majesty and grandeur. He was filled with anger, wonder and pity at the same time. He thought, "What form, what radiance, what strength! If only this king had not swayed from the path of dharma! Not even Indra could have rivaled him in greatness. Alas, Ravana has chosen to bring doom on himself by straying from righteous behavior."

"It does not befit a king of your stature and learning, to carry off another man's wife and hold her captive," Hanuman tried to convince Ravana of his wrongdoing. "Return Sita with all honour to Rama and seek his forgiveness. If not, Rama is bound to kill you and destroy your kingdom."

Ravana was outraged at Hanuman's words. He ordered his men to kill him. Vibheeshana, Ravana's righteous younger brother, intervened. "Brother, it is against our law to kill envoys and messengers. Hurt him in any way you would, but do not kill him."

Ravana accepted Vibheeshana's advice. He asked his men to set fire to Hanuman's most prized possession, his tail.

Lanka set ablaze

The guards carried out Ravana's command with gusto. They dragged the monkey out to the street, doused his tail with oil and set it ablaze. Hanuman then increased his size and made his escape.

"I must leave signs of having come here," said Hanuman to himself. "I must teach Ravana a lesson."

He began jumping from tree to tree, building to building and set fire to whatever came his way. Everything in Lanka, except the tree in Ashoka Vana under which Sita sat, was up in flames.

Hanuman was satisfied with what he had accomplished. He extinguished the fire on his tail by diving into the sea. He was ready to fly back to Kishkinda to give Rama the good tidings. Before leaving Lanka, he once again made his salutations to Sita and took her blessings.

The vanaras rejoice

Hanuman was soon airborne to join his friends on the other shore of the sea. The vanaras were beside themselves with joy when they saw Hanuman flying towards them.

When he told his friends he had found Sita, the vanaras were excited at Hanuman's achievement. They danced, sang, laughed boisterously and made merry.

"Tell us how you found Sita! How does she look? How did Ravana behave? How did you deal with him?" The vanaras bombarded Hanuman with questions. Hanuman who felt humbled by the experience, calmly narrated the events in Lanka to them.

"It is only right that we report your findings to Rama who is anxiously awaiting your return," Jambavan said, after Hanuman finished recounting his visit to Lanka.

All the vanaras proceeded to Kishkinda to give Rama the joyous news of having found Sita.

On the way to Kishkinda, the monkeys saw Sugreeva's most cherished grove, the Madhuvana. The fragrance of flowers, fruits and honey that wafted through the air was too tempting for the monkeys to resist. The vast orchard was well guarded by Sugreeva's maternal uncle Dadhimukha who was its security chief. The simian force was in ecstatic spirit, buoyed by Hanuman's success. They desired to celebrate the accomplishment with fun, frolic and feasting. They sought Angada's permission to enter Madhuvana and partake of the aromatic nectar that hid inside the inviting honeycombs ornamenting several trees. Once inside Madhuvana, the monkeys ran amok in delight. They swung from tree to tree, grabbing and boring their teeth into luscious fruits. They indulged in riotous feasting with singing, dancing, and play, throwing half-eaten fruits at each other. A carnival atmosphere prevailed as the monkeys rejoiced in gay abandon.

Hanuman who could sense their joy supported their celebration and allowed them to drink honey to their hearts content. The vanaras felt encouraged. They pulled down the honeycombs and devoured the honey, intoxicated like seasoned addicts. They drowned themselves in its sweetness and lost their senses. They went berserk with delight and uprooted trees, trampled plants, plucked flowers and scattered them on the lawns.

Dadhimukha was alarmed and angered when he saw the monkeys destroy Sugreeva's prized garden. When he tried to ward them off, the monkeys pounced on him, clawed at him and punched him. Dadhimukha, helpless in the face of the simian rampage, rushed to Kishkinda to inform Sugreeva of the destruction of Madhuvana. Sugreeva, who was in the company of Rama and Lakshmana at that time, was overjoyed upon hearing Dadhimukha's laments! "I am sure Hanuman and his stalwarts, bring us good news. They must have found Sita! For, without succeeding in their mission, they would not indulge in such unruly feasting."

Sugreeva's voice carried his chirpy spirits as he ordered Dadhimukha to return to Madhuvana and ask Hanuman and his army to return to Kishkinda without further delay. "And yes, let the monkeys rejoice. Let them celebrate their success!" he added.

Rama overwhelmed with joy

Dadhimukha returned to Madhuvana and asked the vanaras to immediately hurry to Kishkinda. The monkeys who felt satisfied with all the feasting, followed Hanuman and Angada to Kishkinda.

When the vanaras rejoined Rama, Angada and Jambavan recounted to him their search for Sita, Sampati's tip and the great leap across the sea by Hanuman. The vanara hero who had achieved the incredible feat of crossing the ocean remained humbly silent. He did not utter one word of boast about his rare deed until Rama turned to him and eagerly enquired about Sita.

"I have seen Mother Sita. I met your pure and divine queen. I spoke to the graceful lady who is your wife. I bring you good tidings. Mother Sita is safe even though she is in the midst of the wicked rakshasis," Hanuman spoke, bowing reverentially to Rama.

"Where exactly did you see my beloved Sita? How is she? What did she tell you? Is she being ill-treated by Ravana and the demons in Lanka? Is she looking pale? Has she become thin?" Rama was full of questions to Hanuman.

"Dear Hanuman, please tell me all," Rama was overcome with emotion.

He was overwhelmed by intense waves of pleasure. Tears flowed down his cheeks like a waterfall in deluge as Hanuman narrated his meeting with Sita and the events at Lanka.

"Without you, Mother Sita finds life unbearable. She is holding on to life only to see you again. She is frail and weak without eating. She is living on air and draws energy from the repetition of her Lord's name. Her heart beats for her Lord, Rama.. Rama.. Rama.."

Rama broke down when Hanuman described how he found Sita in Ashoka Vana.

"Mother Sita wants you to rescue her from Ravana as soon as possible. She gave me her crest jewel to hand over to you as a proof of my meeting her." Hanuman then handed over to Rama, the piece of jewelry that Sita had given him.

More tears flowed from Rama's eyes as he saw the piece of jewelry. Rama lauded Hanuman for the monumental task he had accomplished. "Bless you, dear son of Vayu. It is as if I am seeing my Sita through your eyes. None could have done what you have. You have achieved the impossible! I thank you Hanuman for this great service that you have rendered me." Rama hugged Hanuman close to him and said, "High-souled Hanuman, what can I give you for this invaluable task that you have accomplished! I have nothing to offer you today except my heartfelt embrace."

The War

Rama and the vanara force were elated at Hanuman's feat. They began planning their strategy to enter Lanka and rescue Sita. The sons of Dasharatha knew that they had to move fast as time was running out for them. They had only two months within which to land in Lanka, fight Ravana and rescue Sita.

At the appointed auspicious hour, Rama and Lakshmana, accompanied by Sugreeva's army, departed for Lanka, proceeding in the southward direction. The vanara force was in joyous spirits. They were happy to be part of Rama's cause, eager to fight Ravana and secure Sita. They crossed mountains, rivers, cascading falls and forests along the way. The monkeys bathed and played in the water bodies and feasted on the fruits, roots and berries in the jungles. Finally they reached the sea and camped on the seashore.

When Rama saw the ocean waves rise and fall in rhythmic patterns, he was overcome by a wave of nostalgia. He longed to have Sita by his side and once again began to brood over his separation from her. "Time" was not a healer for Rama. Each passing minute was a burden for him because it increased the pain of separation from Sita.

Vibheeshana's advice

Meanwhile, Ravana called an assembly of his ministers. He wanted to take stock of the situation and assess the damage caused to his kingdom by a mere monkey.

"It is evident that Rama is our enemy. How do we strengthen our city and defend ourselves against him?" Ravana addressed his council of ministers.

The ministers praised Ravana and convinced him of his power and strength. "Why should you fear Rama when you have fought greater beings with aplomb? Our warriors are enough to deal with Rama. We have weapons to crush anyone who challenges you."

While the ministers heaped praises on Ravana and his army, Vibheeshana addressed him: "Brother, it is indeed nice to hear what these people say. But it is not good or sensible advice to act upon. I do not desire to flatter you. I wish to save you from grave danger while it is still possible. Rama had done us no harm. If he fought and killed our men in Dandaka forest, he did so only in self-defense. He did it to protect the inhabitants of the forest. Yet you carried his wife away. This unpardonable sin does not befit you. It is against dharma. Even now it is not too late to make amends. Restore Sita to Rama and he will forgive you."

Vibheeshana's pleas to Ravana fell on deaf ears. "No. Never! I will neither restore Sita nor ask Rama for forgiveness," Ravana roared. His eyes turned red with rage and he defiantly announced, "I will fight Rama in battle. Nothing, or no one can make me change my mind."

Vibheeshana who loved his brother persisted in his good counsel. He drew Ravana's attention to the evil portents observed in Lanka since Sita's arrival. Sacrificial fires were engulfed in smoke, reptiles surfaced in the palace kitchens, udders of cows ran dry, flocks of crows gave harsh cries, swarms of vultures hovered over the city and wild animals howled outside the city gates. "The forces of evil have been let lose. It is only wise that you restore Sita to Rama," Vibheeshana pleaded.

However, Ravana was beyond reason. He was not prepared to restore Sita to Rama.

Kumbhakarna, another younger brother, who loved Ravana very much, voiced his honest thoughts to him. "Beloved brother, if you had any grouse against Rama, you should have confronted him with it. You did not act right in carrying Sita away. Actions that flout moral codes of conduct and ethics surely result in sin."

Ravana stubbornly stood his ground.

"Well, if you have made up your mind, I shall fight the sons of Dasharatha and slay them. Victory will be yours, brother," said Kumbhakarna, with an air of finality.

Vibheeshana was steadfast in his resolve. He did not wish to stray into the path of adharma. He extolled the virtues of Rama and sang praises of his valour and might. He made one final effort to make Ravana see sense. "Our defeat is certain if we fight Rama. I beg you brother, return Sita. She rightfully belongs to Rama and no one else. Save yourself from this sinful act and also our people from destruction."

Ravana's son Indrajit scoffed at Vibheeshana whose wisdom was known to equal that of sage Brihaspathi. He ridiculed his uncle for lacking in valour, courage and the spirit of heroism. In angry tones laced with sarcasm, he said, "Being a descendant of the great Pulastya, what shameful words do you utter, uncle! Are you afraid of these mere mortals, Rama and Lakshmana? You insult our lineage by giving father such cowardly advice!"

Vibheeshana responded to Indrajit's tirade with calculated anger, "You are still too young and do not have the capacity to see right from wrong. By goading him on this evil path, you are only ensuring his doom."

Vibheeshana held his ground. Ravana was equally unyielding. "You talk like a coward, brother. If I act upon your words, it would only bring dishonor to the rakshasas." It was obvious that Ravana was lost to reason. Vibheeshana realized there was no place for him in Lanka because he did not wish to be a party to the wrongful deed his brother was intent on committing. He renounced all his possessions and left Lanka to join hands with Rama.

Vibheeshana joins Rama

When Sugreeva noticed Vibheeshana and a few of his armed companions approach their camp, he became apprehensive. He suspected Vibheeshana's intentions and believed he had come as Ravana's spy. While Sugreeva watched Vibheeshana with alertness, the latter stopped midway in flight. He addressed Sugreeva, "I'm Vibheeshana, Ravana's brother. I refused to support my brother in his unholy quest. I have been unable to dissuade Ravana from committing the dishonourable act of coveting Sita. He is unyielding. Four of my close friends and I, have therefore abandoned Lanka and have come to seek refuge in Rama."

Sugreeva conveyed Vibheeshana's words to Rama. At the same time, he cautioned Rama to be careful in dealing with him. Rama promptly called an assembly of the senior members of the vanara force and consulted them on the issue. Angada suggested testing Vibheeshana's trustworthiness. Other vanara elders suggested spying on him to ascertain his true intentions. "One's face mirrors one's inner feelings and nature. I do not see lie and deceit on Vibheeshana's face, nor do I get a hint of it in his voice. Let us accept him as one of us," Hanuman expressed his opinion when Rama asked him to do so.

Rama was delighted to hear Hanuman echo his own sentiments. "Yes. Moreover, how can I refuse to protect one who seeks refuge in me?" The issue was settled without much fuss, to everyone's satisfaction.

Rama received Vibheeshana with great love. Vibheeshana and his friends prostrated at Rama's feet. The pious and noble brother of Ravana then apprised Rama of the events in Lanka that led to his departure from the kingdom. He also explained how even Kumbhakarna disapproved of Ravana's act, but chose to stand by him out of loyalty to his brother. Vibheeshana said, "Though I love my brother, I cannot take sides with adharma. Inspite of my best efforts I failed to persuade Ravana to restore Sita to you and seek your pardon."

Rama could see it was not an easy decision to forsake one's own brother for the cause of dharma. Yet, here was Vibheeshana who acted with courage at the risk of being misunderstood for deserting his brother. Rama embraced Vibheeshana. He also promised to crown him as the king of Lanka after fighting the war with Ravana and defeating him. In the presence of the vanara forces, Rama carried out the consecration of Vibheeshana with holy water from the sea.

Meanwhile Ravana made an attempt to win over Sugreeva to his side. One evening, Sugreeva saw a parrot flying across the sky. It landed on his shoulder. It was a rakshasa by name Shuka in disguise. He was a messenger from Ravana who incited Sugreeva to desert Rama and return to Kishkinda with his vanara army. Sugreeva spurned Ravana's offer of friendship and sent away the envoy from Lanka.

Rama prays to the ocean

Rama, along with Vibheeshana and the vanaras strategized for the war. They first had to find a way to cross the mighty ocean to reach Lanka.

Vibheeshana then suggested to Rama to seek the help of the ocean to enable them cross it. "Since King Sagara of the Ikshvaku linage was instrumental in digging the ocean, thus giving it life, the ocean will surely help you, Rama," said Vibheeshana. His advice appealed to Rama and the vanara chief.

Rama prayed to the ocean to provide a passage so that he and his army could walk across to Lanka. For three days he prayed and there was no response from the ocean. This made Rama angry. He said, "If well-meaning sentiments and virtues such as patience, politeness, pity, and plain speaking are perceived as signs of meekness, let me show the ocean what I can do!"

Rama then threatened to dry up the ocean and cause all the creatures dwelling in it to disappear. He picked up his bow and took aim at the ocean."If you do not grant us a passage, I know how to make one," he said, in a quiet yet menacing voice. As Rama strung his bow, the world was plunged in darkness. All the natural forces began to display abnormal behavior.

It was then that a splendorous figure rose from the ocean. He was the lord of the ocean, who stood reverentially before Rama with folded hands. He pointed out to Rama that the five elements had to obey the eternal laws of nature. "There is a way to travel across the ocean," he said. He suggested that Rama should build a long causeway to connect the two shores. "But rest assured that the creatures of the sea will not harm your force. The alligators, sharks and all other animals that inhabit my realms, will remain non- aggressive. You may carry on the building of your bridge without fear of being attacked by them," the lord of the ocean promised. Rama accepted the suggestion and lowered his bow.

A squirrel's contribution

He approached Nala, the vanara engineer, to build the giant causeway across the sea. Nala, the son of the divine architect Vishwakarma, was only too happy to oblige Rama. The monkeys, under the watchful eyes of Nala, transported huge boulders and dropped them into the sea to build the bridge to Lanka.

Rama was very happy to see the high energy level, passion and dedication of his army towards constructing the bridge. Many forest animals and birds were watching the vanaras at work. Among them was a squirrel that was devoted to Rama. Though small in size, it too wanted to chip in its bit towards his cause. It carried small pebbles in its mouth and dropped them into the sea alongside the boulders. The squirrel repeated this continuously and effortlessly. A monkey who saw its activity mocked at it and asked it to stay away, saying it would die if it came under the boulder or feet of the vanara army. Upon this, all the other monkeys and bears joined in ridiculing the squirrel and laughed at it. The squirrel was driven to tears but it continued to pick the pebbles and told the vanara force that it too wished to help them in getting Sita free from the clutches of Ravana. Rama was overwhelmed to see its devotion. As he watched this sight, the squirrel which was now carrying a bigger pebble stumbled and fell from a height. Rama moved swiftly and caught it on time. The squirrel felt overjoyed at Rama's touch. Rama stroked it lovingly and gently dropped it to the ground. It is widely believed that the stripes we see on a squirrel's back are the result of Rama's caressing stroke on this squirrel's back. Rama then showed the monkey army how the pebbles that it had thrown into the sea served to fill the gap between two boulders. He made them realize that its contribution was as big as that of any other member of his army.

Walk on the sea link

Meanwhile the work on the bridge made brisk progress. When it was finally ready, Vibheeshana and the huge vanara army set out on it for a long walk to the island fortress of Lanka. While Hanuman carried Rama on his shoulder, Angada took Lakshmana on his. The vanaras raised victory cries and marched ahead, eager to battle. Soon they reached Mount Suvela on the seashore and rested on it for the night.

The following morning, Rama took a good look at Lanka, resting majestically atop the Trikuta Mountain. The city of Lanka was beautiful and prosperous. Rama felt sad that for one man's folly the entire population of Lanka was going to suffer. At the same time, he reminded himself that he should focus on overcoming Ravana. Sugreeva marshalled his troops and systematically organized their formation in preparation for war.

When Ravana learned of Rama having crossed the sea with Sugreeva's forces, he sent two of his ministers, Suka and Sarana to penetrate the enemy camp. He ordered them to spy on their foe and assess their strength, their numbers and the weaponry at their disposal. The demon ministers entered Sugreeva's army, disguised as monkeys. But Vibheeshana recognized them and took them to Rama. They confessed to being spies sent by Ravana. Rama set them free with a message for Ravana, "Tell your king that tomorrow's dawn will spell doom for him and his grand city of Lanka."

Suka and Sarana, while conveying Rama's message to Ravana, extolled the virtues of Rama. "Rama, Lakshmana, Sugreeva and Vibheeshana, are very virtuous. Moreover, they have such matchless weapons, that we do not stand any chance of winning against them. In fact, Rama alone is capable of destroying Lanka. O king of Lanka, wisdom therefore lies in making peace with Rama by restoring Sita to him."

Ravana remained unyielding. "Even if gods asked me to return Sita, I would not do so!" The king of Lanka was only interested in getting the information that the two ministers had gathered from the rival camp. Suka and Sarana duly gave Ravana a detailed report on the organization of the vanara army, highlighting the skills and strengths of each commander. Once he received this information, he expelled the two ministers from his court for having praised the enemy forces. He dispatched yet other ogres to Rama's field to carry on espionage.

Ravana's deceit

Ravana was disturbed by the reports he heard of the advancing enemy. He tried to induce fear in Sita to get her to submit to his overtures. He commanded Vidyujjihva, his court magician to produce an illusory head of Rama. At the behest of Ravana, Vidyujjihva brandished the head before Sita at Ashoka Vana as proof that Rama had been killed.

Sita burst into tears upon seeing Rama's head, and soon fainted. When she recovered, she lamented her fate and spoke with disdain of astrologers who had predicted long life for Rama. She shot a fiery glance at Ravana who urged her to submit to him now that Rama was dead. "Kill me right away and let my body be placed alongside Rama," she wailed. As Ravana was threatening Sita, a messenger arrived from his court, bringing news that required him to act urgently. As soon as Ravana left Sita and Ashoka Vana, Rama's head too disappeared!

An ogress by name Sarama took pity on Sita who was distraught with grief on learning of Rama's death. She comforted Sita and disclosed to her the fact that Rama was well and alive. Sarama revealed to Sita that the head was an illusory one created by the court magician. In addition, Sarama kept Sita apprised of the proceedings in Ravana's court. She informed Sita that Ravana's mother Kaikasi, had urged her son to restore Sita with due honour, to Rama. "But Ravana will listen to no one. Virtuous Sita, you must not let your confidence in Rama fail you. Very soon, he will defeat Ravana and take you back with him," Sarama consoled Sita with these words.

A grandfather's advice

Meanwhile, Lanka resonated with the sounds of kettledrums and conches. Rama's forces were closing in on Lanka, and were close to the city's outskirts. Ravana addressed his council of ministers reprimanding them for being intimidated by Rama's supposed prowess. He reminded them of their own expertise and heroism. When Malyavan, Ravana's maternal grandfather heard him speak with such confidence, he advised him. "It is wise to go for war if you are superior to your adversary in strength and skill. But if you see yourself losing, or if you are equally matched with your enemy, it is best, and in everyone's interest, to make peace. You would be wise to restore Sita to Rama and make peace with him."

Ravana stubbornly persisted. Malyavan continued to address him, "Ravana, realize that you have immunity from death at the hands of gods, demons and yakshas. But you are now facing human beings, monkeys and bears against whom you are not protected. Do you not see several bad omens that we have been observing in Lanka for some time now? Give up your evil design while there is still time. Moreover, we firmly believe that Rama is none other than Vishnu in human form. So there is no way you can conquer him. Make peace with him, Ravana and save yourself and our people from certain death and destruction."

Ravana who was firmly rooted on the path of ruin scoffed at his grandfather and accused him of having joined forces with Rama. He then posted his ablest commanders at the four gates of Lanka to thwart the vanara army's entrance into the city.

Rama's message to Ravana

Rama, along with Lakshmana, Vibheeshana and Sugreeva climbed the vantage point on Mount Suvela to assess the happenings in Lanka. As they were surveying the environs of Lanka, Sugreeva spotted Ravana on the terrace of the tallest tower in the city. On sudden impulse, the vanara king took one long leap and landed on the terrace, taking Ravana by surprise. He knocked down Ravana's crown and gave him a push. One moment Ravana was down;

next moment he bounced back on his feet and took Sugreeva by his neck. The two wrestled for a while. Then as Ravana came closer, Sugreeva bounded back to Mount Suvela as the vanara brigade raised a war cry.

Battle cries were heard in Lanka to the beating of drums and trumpets. However, before beginning an onslaught on Ravana's forces, Rama sent Angada with a message to the Lord of Lanka. "Oh great sinner, your end is approaching. Rama is at your fort gate, ready to fight you. Haughty king, if you love your life, if you are repentant for your evil deed, restore Sita to him. Beg Rama's forgiveness. He is merciful."

Angada continued to deliver Rama's message to Ravana, "The choice is yours; either fight Rama and die in battle, or surrender to him and seek his mercy. But if we know you well, you would elect to fight. Bid your family and citizens farewell. Have a last look at your beautiful Lanka which you have ruined by sheer arrogance. Vibheeshana who is just and righteous will be crowned king."

Ravana became wrathful on hearing Angada's words. He called out to his men and ordered: "Grab him and kill him!"

As Ravana's guards made to seize Angada, the monkey rose up in the sky. He lifted the two guards, one in each hand, soared high, and flung them down.

Meanwhile the vanara army surrounded Lanka on all sides. Rama then allocated his forces to fight Ravana. He assigned a specific task to each of his stalwart vanara commanders.

The war begins

The battle between the two sides began in all ferocity. It raged unabated through the day and continued into the night. Horses galloped with riders and elephants marched with soldiers mounted on them. All kinds of weapons flew in every direction, each meeting its target. Soldiers who had fallen, cried loud in pain and agony. Lanka's fertile, brown earth turned red with the blood bath. Both sides witnessed heavy loss of life.

Angada took on Indrajit and overpowered him. He killed his charioteer and horses, wounded Indrajit and smashed his chariot. Fatigued from the onslaught, Ravana's son disappeared from the battlefield. Angada was applauded by his vanara compatriots for defeating Indrajit. However, because Indrajit had been granted a boon by Brahma that he could become invisible at will, the enemy presumed he had fled the field in fear.

Indrajit who was enfeebled by Angada, fumed and frothed at this insult. He remained invisible, and shot serpent darts at Rama and Lakshmana. The brothers who became bound by the darts, fell down and became immobile. Indrajit, who believed them to be dead, boasted about how he had successfully defeated and killed them. He then pierced all the other vanaras with his arrows and struck terror in the monkey camp. The vanaras too thought the Dasharatha siblings to be dead, and began to mourn them. Vibheeshana, however, consoled Sugreeva and the vanara force, and asked them not to despair, and remain optimistic. He asked them to protect the brothers until they regained consciousness. "Rest assured that Rama is not going to die. The brave and courageous sons of Dasharatha have only fainted. It is just a matter of time before they recover from the swoon."

Indrajit who was convinced he had killed Rama and Lakshmana, conveyed the news to Ravana. The king of Lanka was elated at his sons's feat and hugged Indrajit.

He then called Trijata the demoness who was guarding Sita in Ashoka Vana. He asked Trijata to convey to Sita the news of the death of Rama and Lakshmana. He also asked Trijata to take Sita on the Pushpaka Vimana for her to see their dead bodies. Trijata carried out Ravana's orders. Sita was heartbroken when she saw Rama and Lakshmana lie ensnared, pierced by countless arrows and darts. She looked frail and wretched as she sobbed inconsolably.

Trijata, the good-natured ogre, immediately reasoned with Sita. She convinced her that Rama and Lakshmana were unconscious, but not dead. "If indeed they were dead, there would be pell-mell among his army. But look there, the monkeys appear to be guarding the brothers. Why would anybody protect the dead? Look at the faces of the fallen heroes – there is no pallor in them to indicate death. Do you not see their faces radiate a spark? Trust me O princess of Mithila, I would not lie to you, for you have conquered me by your noble disposition. Rama and Lakshmana are invincible and even the combined forces of the gods and demons cannot vanquish them." Sita prayed for Trijata's words to be true.

As Sugreeva and his army grieved over Rama and Lakshmana, Rama regained consciousness. When he rose and saw Lakshmana lie lifeless, disconsolate. "With my beloved brother gone, of what use would my very life be to me?"

Rama felt devastated upon seeing Lakshmana lie inert, bathed in blood, arrows all over him. He felt defeated at the hands of destiny. He thanked Sugreeva and his army profusely for rendering him every possible help in locating Sita. He asked all of them to go their way since all was now lost.

Garuda to the rescue

As Sugreeva was pondering over the turn of events, they were interrupted by lightning and thunder. The sky was overcast with dense clouds and a strong gust of wind whipped up dust and fallen leaves in its wake. Uprooted trees fell into the sea causing alarm among the marine creatures. Suddenly, Garuda, the mount of Vishnu, appeared before them. When the serpents, in the form of arrows binding Rama and Lakshmana, saw their arch enemy Garuda approaching them, they immediately slithered away in fear. Garuda wiped the faces of Rama and Lakshmana, wished them good luck and embraced them. By the mere touch of Garuda, the brothers were restored their powers.

As Garuda took leave of them, he cautioned them to remain vigilant against the ogres on the battle field. "They are treacherous by nature and will take recourse to devious means to win. Rama, you have done well to kill most of the males in Lanka, except for the aged and youngsters. You will succeed in vanquishing Ravana and getting Sita back."

The battle resumes

Once again there was jubilation in the monkey camp. A great battle followed. When Ravana lost his most capable contingent of warriors one after another, he himself appeared on the battlefield to face the enemy. It was a fierce clash of goliaths. Ravana struck the monkey force with thousands of arrows. Many of them lost their lives. The monkey brigade feared Ravana and sought shelter in Rama. Rama was ready with his bow to strike terror among the forces of Ravana. The heroic

Lakshmana wanted to take on Ravana. Rama acceded to his request. He cautioned Lakshmana to be wary of the demon's moves, keeping in mind his strengths and weaknesses. "Ever be alert, keep your eyes focused and defend yourself well with the weapons you wield," Rama advised. The brothers embraced and Lakshmana marched ahead to confront Ravana.

The battle between Ravana and Lakshmana raged relentlessly. Arrows flew in a continuous volley, wounding both of them. Ravana finally used the javelin that Brahma had presented to him. He sent it flying at Lakshmana. Though Lakshmana saw the weapon approach him and tried to counter it, the javelin had done the damage. It pierced Lakshmana on the chest and gravely wounded him.

Hanuman who saw Lakshmana fall down unconscious, darted ferociously towards Ravana. He dealt the demon a heavy blow on his chest. As Ravana slumped to the ground, blood splattered from his ears, eyes and mouth. Hanuman picked up the unconscious Lakshmana and carried him to Rama. Soon enough, both, Lakshmana and Ravana regained consciousness and were ready for combat. Hanuman asked Rama to perch himself on his shoulder and fight the Lord of Lanka. As Rama rushed towards Ravana, he told the demon king that no matter which god or deity he approached, defeat and death at his hands was certain. "While you cannot escape from me after having offended me, your sons and grandsons will meet the same fate at the hands of Lakshmana."

Ravana's anger increased several times on hearing Rama's words. He hit Hanuman with arrows that were potentially more dangerous and harmful. When Rama saw the wounds on Hanuman, he was enraged. He smashed Ravana's chariot, and then with a vengeance, shot an arrow at Ravana that pierced the demon's chest. Ravana fainted from its impact. Rama asked Ravana to return to his palace, take rest and come back the following day to continue the battle.

Ravana's chariot was shattered to pieces. His horse and charioteer were killed. Rama had handled the situation in a judicious manner and added insult to injury. Ravana's ego was hurt.

Kumabhakarna

Ravana recalled the words of Brahma who had warned him against human beings. He recollected an event from the past. King Anaranya of the Ikshvaku lineage once cursed Ravana saying that one of his descendents would be the cause of his death in battle. "Perhaps, Rama is the one at whose hands I'm fated to die!"

Ravana who was visibly shaken by this confrontation with Rama, recalled other incidents from the past. He had incurred the wrath of Goddess Uma. When Ravana once lifted Mount Kailasa, Uma cursed him saying that a woman would be the ultimate cause of his death. Nalakubera, the son of Kubera, and Brahma too, had cursed Ravana with death if he cast evil designs upon any woman. Ravana recalled another incident when he had ridiculed Nandiswara for resembling a monkey in looks. Nandiswara cursed Ravana saying that his destruction would be brought about by monkeys who would fight him in battle.

Ravana summoned his ministers and asked them to wake up the slumbering Kumbhakarna. It was a tall task to wake up the sleeping giant before his due time. The demon who was ordained to sleep for six months at a stretch had gone to sleep barely a month ago. The ogres wondered how they would wake him up. They proceeded to his grand mansion located in a cave in the subterranean region. They carried with them humongous mounds of food, garlands and perfumes. When they entered his chamber they were greeted by the sounds of his sonorous snoring. The ogres staggered and stumbled as they were pushed by the force of the wind that blew from Kumbhakarna's nostrils as he breathed. They tried to tickle his sense of smell and rouse him from sleep, using the aroma of meat and fragrance of flowers and incense. They played loudly on drums, trumpets and other musical instruments to wake him up. But to no avail. The ogres then beat, thrashed and struck him all over his body, tore at his hair, bit his ears and nose, hoping to awaken him.

Finally Kumbhakarna woke up when a huge herd of elephants was made to walk over him as he lay stretched in sleep. Kumbhakarna woke up, unhurt. He roared, ravenous from hunger. He devoured enormous quantities of meat of different kinds. When his hunger was sated, he demanded to know the reason for being woken up. He proceeded to his brother's palace when he was informed that Ravana had summoned him.

The vanaras ran here and there in a chaotic manner upon seeing the gigantic figure of Kumbhakarna. He appeared menacing as he walked the streets of Lanka. Rama wished to know from Vibeeshana the identity of this massive ogre. Vibheeshana responded by telling Rama that he was one of Ravana's brothers who had defeated Indra and Yama. Vibheeshana also gave Rama a brief history of Kumbhakarna. Kumbhakarna, the most gigantic of the ogres, had a voracious appetite, even as an infant. He would devour and digest, thousands of creatures. He once destroyed a tusk of Airavata, the celestial elephant of Indra. He then delivered a smarting blow to Indra. The gods including Indra feared that there would be no creatures left on earth if Kumbhakarna gobbled them at the rate he did. They approached Brahma for a solution to the threat posed by the colossus. Brahma cast a spell on Kumbhakarna to remain eternally buried in sleep. Ravana intervened on behalf of his brother. Brahma relented and modified his curse. He said that Kumbhakarna would sleep continuously for six months, following which he would enjoy one day of wakefulness.

Ravana briefed Kumbhakarna about the heavy casualties his army had faced in battle. He urged his brother to take on Rama and the vanara forces. Ravana embraced his brother and adorned him with ornaments before the latter left for battle. Once again there were ill omens as the demon of massive proportions led his forces to battle.

There was pell-mell among the bears and monkeys as Kumbhakarna struck terror in them by his mere presence. A stampede ensued among the monkey troops as they saw Kumbhakarna make towards them. Angada rebuked them saying that even their wives would scoff at them for being cowardly and beating retreat. The simians who felt ashamed on hearing Angada's words, returned to fight, even if it meant dying in battle. They lifted mountains and peaks, uprooted huge trees and hurled them at Kumbhakarna. Ravana's brother simply intercepted them all and split them with little effort, in mid air.

The prodigious Hanuman, struck Kumbhakarna a powerful blow by lifting up a mammoth mountain peak and hurling it at him. The demon reeled under its impact and blood gushed from his body. He got up with redoubled vigour and dealt Hanuman a piercing punch with his sharp pike on his breast. The son of Vayu was rendered powerless. When the vanara army saw their most indomitable leader fall down injured, they once again began to withdraw from the arena. The mighty Nila, one of their principal commanders, restored their confidence. The monkeys relentlessly pounded Kumbhakarna with trees, crags, peaks and fists, but to no avail. Angada put up a courageous fight only to fall unconscious with injuries. The demon brother of Ravana was too powerful for the vanara force. They were killed in large numbers and greater numbers lay grievously wounded. They were gripped with fear as they saw some of their great leaders fall under Kumbhakarna's brutal offensive. Sugreeva too fell senseless on the field. The ogre captured the fallen Sugreeva and started walking towards Lanka.

Hanuman, who bounced back from Kumbhakarna's ferocious blow, buoyed the sagging spirit of the warring monkeys. Meanwhile, Sugreeva recovered consciousness as he was being carried by Kumbhakarna on his back. The king of the monkeys, clawed at, and tore the demon's ears and bit off his nose. Kumbhakarna who was writhing in pain, flung Sugreeva to the ground. As soon as Sugreeva hit the earth, he leaped into the air and joined hands with Rama, who now entered the battlefield, to fight Kumbhakarna.

As the ogre of mammoth size began to devour the monkeys by the thousands, Lakshmana escalated his own confrontation with greater vigour and fury. Kumbhakarna now saw Lakshmana's fighting skills and abilities in a new light, with more respect. Yet, he insisted on fighting Rama alone, and defeating him. His words reeked of arrogance as he said, "It is Rama alone I seek to fight and kill. When he is slayed, the entire vanara force will be destroyed." Kumbhakarna then rushed towards Rama, raining a torrent of weapons on him. Rama countered these missiles with the bow of Rudra, rendering Kumbhakarna's arsenal, powerless. When Kumbhakarna heard the twang of Rama's bow, he lunged forward laughing hideously. He claimed he would devour Rama, as effortlessly as he had, members of the simian troop.

Vibheeshana, who was seething with anger at Kumbhakarna's words, charged ahead of Rama, to fight his elder brother. Kumbhakarna who saw his brother's eagerness to fight him, addressed him with affection, "Beloved brother, you are the only one amongst us who has dared to stand on the side of truth and righteousness. You have sought Rama's refuge and by his grace you will reign over Lanka. But for now, I who am engaged in battle and see neither friend nor foe, beg you to move away from my line of firing. For, I do not wish to kill you."

It wrenched Vibheeshana's heart to hear his brother's words. His eyes welled up with tears as he moved away from the line of action. He watched with an aching heart, the clash between his brother and Rama. A violent encounter followed. Kumbhakarna intercepted the missiles rained on him by Rama. The scion of Ikshvaku then axed the mighty demon's right arm which bore semblance to a huge mountain peak in weight and magnitude. As his gargantuan arm fell down, it crushed thousands of monkeys under its weight. The surviving monkeys stood by their dead fellowmates and witnessed the most gruesome encounter between Rama and the demon. Rama soon severed Kumbhakarna's left arm as the latter raised it to hurl a weapon at him. More vanaras lost their lives, crushed under the weight of the ogre's second arm. Rama sheared off each limb of Kumbhakarna, and finally the valiant ogre's head rolled down, chopped off by Rama's missile. Several mansions, gates and defense walls of Lanka lay waste under the burden of the falling skull. There was great cheering among the gods, Gandharvas, sages and celestial beings as Kumbhakarna lay annihilated.

Ravana's grief

Ravana was beside himself with sorrow on hearing of Kumbhakarna's death. Kumbhakarna, his right hand had fallen prey to Rama and the demon king of Lanka was certain his own end was near. "What shall I do with this kingdom, or with Sita, after you, my dear brother, have departed from this world!" he cried. "I do not even wish to remain alive any longer. I rue that I did not heed the sagely council of Vibheeshana. I have brought calamity upon myself and on our entire kinfolk, as he had rightly pointed out."

Trisira, a son of Ravana, was appalled to hear his father speak in defeated terms. He chided Ravana for wallowing in sorrow and self-pity. He goaded his father to pick himself up and resume fighting. He asked him not to feel overwhelmed by the situation and turn chicken-hearted which was most unbecoming of a king and warrior of his class. He instilled confidence in Ravana by recounting to him his skills and abilities, of his potent power with which he was capable of winning over the three worlds. Trisira, took it upon himself to defeat Rama. The spirits of the Ravana's army was bolstered when they heard Trisira speak with such valour and courage. Ravana gave orders to Trisira, his other sons and brothers to prepare afresh for another campaign against Rama.

The renewed struggle once again witnessed a terrible blood bath. Both sides suffered heavy loss of lives. The battle field had turned into a vast mound of debris, ridden with fallen mountains, uprooted trees and flesh and limbs of mortally wounded creatures. As the battle escalated to a feverish pitch, Angada, Nila and Hanuman, slayed the sons and brothers of Ravana, including the daring Trisira.

The fall of Trisira, led Atikaya to take up cudgels on behalf of Ravana. Atikaya who has mastered the Vedas, equalled his father Ravana in might. He was proficient in the use of mystic missiles, a blessing that he had obtained by propitiating Brahma. Atikaya challenged Rama to a fight, whereupon Lakshmana stretched his bow to strike him. Atikaya who was arrogance personified, addressed Lakshmana: "You are still too young to fight me. I am invincible. You are no match for me, for I am Kaala, or Time itself. There is none who can overpower or kill me. If you cherish your life, retreat from battle and let Rama face me."

Lakshmana became furious on hearing Atikaya speak with such haughtiness. He shot back at him: "If you are as powerful as you claim, let your actions bespeak your skills. Just as a small-statured Vishnu covered all the three worlds in three strides, I too, though young, will deliver you to the abode of Yama."

The verbal altercations between Atikaya and Lakshmana, was followed by a deadly clash between them. According to a boon granted to Atikaya by Brahma, this son of Ravana could not be destroyed by any weapon except the missile presided over by Brahma. At the height of the fight between the stalwarts, the wind God appeared before Lakshmana and prompted him to use the Brahmastra on Atikaya. Lakshmana did as advised and severed the demon's head.

Indrajit's Brahmastra

Ravana grieved for Atikaya as he did for his other deceased sons and siblings. But he stubbornly stood his ground and expressed his desire to see the war through to its conclusion. He feared for the safety of Lanka and gave orders for greater fortification of the city, especially of Ashoka Vana where Sita was held captive.

The young and spirited Indrajit, Ravana's eldest and favourite son, boosted his father's floundering spirits. He assured him that none could ever vanquish their lot so long as he, Indrajit himself, was alive. He bragged about his own skills on the basis of Indra's exceptionally powerful arrows that he possessed. Indrajit prepared to confront Rama and Lakshmana after duly propitiating Agni, the God of Fire. He then made himself invisible and began systematic destruction of the vanara force. The monkeys stood firm and brave, facing Indrajit in invisible form and embracing death for Rama's cause.

The battle progressed. Indrajit invoked the dreaded Brahmastra. In order to show due respect to the potent weapon presided over by Brahma, Rama and Lakshmana willed themselves to be bound by it. When Indrajit saw the brothers had fallen and were lying motionless, he rejoiced and claimed victory over them. He left for Lanka to convey the joyous news to his father – of the defeat of the sons of Dasharatha at his hands.

The entire vanara army despaired on seeing the heroes fallen. Vibheeshana, however, urged them to remain confident and courageous. He dispelled the fears they entertained by telling them that Rama and Lakshmana had opted to remain unconscious as a mark of respect to Brahma whose missile had been used by Indrajit to overpower and overwhelm them. Hanuman and Vibheeshana then set about comforting the injured among their troop. Jambavan, the wise bear also lay wounded in the clash. When he heard Hanuman's voice he called out to him and said, "Hanuman, you alone can help the monkeys and our wounded vanara force in the war against Indrajit. You must use your insurmountable skills and fly out to the Sanjeevani Mountain to bring, four life-saving and medicinal herbs from there. These herbs are capable of restoring the dead to life, healing injuries and restoring the body to its original glory."

Hanuman felt inspired by Jambavan's words and by the faith the elderly bear reposed in his abilities. The mighty Hanuman stood towering over the Trikuta Mountain, ready to take off on yet another mission that had been entrusted to him. One huge purge, and Hanuman was air borne, on his way to cover thousands of yojanas to reach the Himalayas. When the herbaceous plants saw Hanuman approach them, they hid themselves from his view! The resolute Hanuman, in his inimitable fashion, gave a tremendous roar and seized Sanjeevani Mountain with one swift movement of his hand. He carried the treasured peak to bring back to life his entire army of vanaras and bears. The fragrance from the herbs infused new life into the simian army and they resumed their battle against the ogres. Meanwhile, Ravana, as part of his war tactics, disposed off into the sea, the dead ogres belonging to his army. He did this to ensure that the enemy would not have a count of the remaining demons. They would therefore, not be able to gauge the strength of his army in terms of their numbers.

Makaraksa killed by Lakshmana

The army of monkeys re-entered Lanka with burning torches. The ogres who were positioned at the strategic gates of Lanka, fled upon seeing the rejuvenated monkey force. Meanwhile, the monkeys got busy destroying Lanka, setting fire to everything that came their way. Lanka was doused in fire. As the battle raged, Angada killed several of the ogre commanders. Kumba and Nikumba, sons of Kumbhakarna were killed by Sugreeva and Hanuman. When Ravana heard of their deaths, he ordered Khara's son Makaraksa to fight the monkeys. All kinds of missiles were hurled and brave warriors on both sides met their bloody end. Many of the injured monkeys could not withstand the volley of weapons discharged by Makaraksa and his army. They fled the field in fear. When Rama noticed his vanara force run helter-skelter, he intercepted the hail of shafts that flew from the enemy camp. An overconfident and conceited Makaraksa, challenged Rama to fight him. He bragged that it was only a matter of time before he made mincemeat of Rama. He dared Rama, eager to avenge the death of his father at Janasthana. A close encounter followed between them. As Rama twanged his bow, its sound reverberated throughout the battlefield like a loud thunderclap. All the heavenly beings watched the combat as the titans inflicted deep gashes on each other. Rama soon killed Makaraksa's charioteer and shattered his chariot to pieces. Makaraksa who was incensed by this, flung his pike at Rama. In a split second, Rama smashed the demon's pike into several pieces. Makaraksa charged at Rama like an enraged bull. The son of Dasharatha used his all-powerful weapon on the demon. It pierced Makaraksa's heart and tore it asunder; life soon ebbed out of the youngster.

Lakshmana slays Indrajit

Ravana and Indrajit had elaborate consultation following the fall of Makaraksa. Ravana commanded Indrajit to take on Rama and Lakshmana in battle, maintaining visible or invisible form. Indrajit offered oblations to the fire and after performing the necessary rituals, left for war. With his extraordinary strength and skill he had conquered even Indra in combat and had never lost a war. "These sons of Dasharatha are mere mortals. I shall easily destroy them and win this war for my father", Indrajit said to himself. He immediately assumed an invisible form and proceeded to the battlefield. Arrows, spears and missiles rained down upon Rama's army. Lakshmana sought to put an end to Indrajit by using the mystic missile of Brahma upon him. Rama reprimanded him for the rash action, saying, "It is not fair to destroy the entire army of rakshasas by using this potent missile, when it is Indrajit who fights us by making himself invisible. Let us, in unison, bring all our other weapons to bear upon him and destroy him."

The shrewd Indrajit divined the brothers' intentions. He immediately used his conjuring skills to good effect. He created an illusory image of Sita and placed it on his chariot. He then directed his army of ogres to surround the chariot and wield weapons at 'Sita'. It was his intention to hoodwink Rama and Lakshmana into believing Sita had been killed by them. Indrajit put his plan to action when he saw the monkey force rush towards his chariot. He pulled Sita by her hair and struck her hard. Sita, pained by the blow and tug at her hair, called out to Rama to rescue her. Hanuman's heart bled when he saw the brutality that Indrajit inflicted upon her. He began a tirade against Indrajit and rushed at him. The simian troop followed him. As Hanuman looked on in horror, Indrajit split the illusory Sita, asunder. Hanuman was struck with grief and he rushed towards the enemy force with murderous intent and ferocity. He hurled a huge rock upon Indrajit's chariot. The charioteer who saw the rock coming rode the vehicle to safety. Nevertheless, thousands of ogres lay crushed under the rock as it hit ground. The monkeys felt encouraged by Hanuman's act. They darted towards Indrajit. The vanaras created havoc in the battlefield. Hanuman then proceeded to meet Rama to inform him of Sita's demise at the hands of Indrajit.

Rama fainted on hearing of Sita's tragic end. Lakshmana consoled him and prepared himself to kill Indrajit and avenge Sita's death. However, when Vibheeshana heard the news, he immediately restored order in Rama's army and turned his attention to Lakshmana and Rama who had fallen down unconscious. He informed the brothers that Sita could not be dead and it was nothing but magic performed by Indrajit. Vibeeshana allayed Rama's fears by saying, "It is merely an illusion that Indrajit has created to cause chaos among our forces. I beseech you Rama, to please send Lakshmana to fight Indrajit and put an end to him."

Vibheeshana continued talking to Rama, "Indrajit has gone to Nikumbhila sanctuary to perform a pre-war ritual and pour oblations into the fire. According to a boon that he has been granted by Brahma, if he is allowed to conclude this ritual successfully, no force on earth can destroy him. It is only wise that you immediately dispatch Lakshmana to kill Indrajit before he offers oblations to the fire deity."

As Rama, Lakshmana and the vanara forces proceeded to Nikumbhila, Vibheeshana spelled out a course of action for Rama to follow to bring Indrajit out of his invisible form. Rama and his army acted upon Vibheeshana's plan and began to shower arrows upon the demon army so that at least some of them would hit their invisible target – Indrajit. Lanka was in the throes of a great battle that saw weapons race with great speed in every direction. The demons grew desperate as the monkeys bombarded them with massive crags and massifs. Indrajit's army became dispirited with the onslaught by the vanaras. When Indrajit was informed of this, he was so troubled that he abandoned the rites midway, to join the battle, without concluding the ritual he had begun. When the rakshasa force saw Indrajit's preparedness to resume fighting, they hovered around him. Hanuman immediately uprooted a gargantuan tree and flung it at the charging demons, creating havoc among them. A vicious clash of the rival armies followed. Indrajit rode on his chariot right in front of Hanuman and rained weapons upon him. As Hanuman and Indrajit were engaged in a scuffle, Vibheeshana directed Lakshmana to slay Indrajit as the latter hastened to kill Hanuman. He also pointed out to Lakshmana, a banyan tree where Indrajit would offer oblations to the fire spirit. "Act fast, Lakshmana," Vibheeshana spurred him. "Intercept him now, before he pours the oblations into the fire. This is your only chance to overpower and kill him. Hurry O Lakshmana before he reaches the banyan tree."

Lakshmana immediately challenged Indrajit to a duel. Indrajit noticed Vibheeshana standing next to Lakshmana when he accepted Lakshmana's challenge. Indrajit rebuked his uncle and scorned at him for being disloyal to his own kinsman and joining hands with the enemy. Vibheeshana reiterated his stand to Indrajit, recounting Ravana's misdeeds: "Your father has done everything possible to ensure doom for himself. He had mindlessly slaughtered seers, forcefully carried another man's wife and coveted what is not rightfully his. I abandoned him for these very reasons only after advising him on a number of occasions against pursuing these evils designs. Unfortunately, your end today is certain, and nothing, or no one can change that!"

A titanic battle ensued between Indrajit who rode on a chariot, and Lakshmana who was perched on Hanuman's back. It was a fight between equals. As soon as Vibheeshana sensed Indrajit was becoming desperate, he advised Lakshmana to strike him. Lakshmana acted with great speed. He first slayed Indrajit's charioteer and then smashed the chariot to pieces. Finally he severed Indrajit's head.

The heavens rejoiced at Indrajit's fall. There was music, dance and merriment accompanied by bands and other musical instruments. Victory cries reverberated throughout the city. Rama felt elated at Lakshmana's accomplishment. All the injured vanaras were treated with the herbs and healed.

Ravana's rage

Ravana felt shattered on hearing of Indrajit's death at the hands of Lakshmana. Nothing mattered to him any more. His fury amplified and he desired to avenge his son's death and that of all his kinsmen. He brandished his sword and made towards Ashoka Vana. He loudly announced to his ministers that he would seek his revenge by killing Sita. Sita trembled with fear when she saw a blood-thirsty Ravana approach her, sword in hand and fibrillating with malevolent energy. She wondered, "Is it that he has come to kill me because I have not surrendered to his obnoxious desire? Could it be that he has killed my beloved Rama and is now here to make me his consort! I guess I deserve this punishment for not having heeded the noble Hanuman's wise counsel. Did he not offer to carry me on his back and unite me with Rama? Had I listened to him, I would not have had to see these days! Mother Kausalya would be devastated to know that her only son is dead, killed by Ravana." As Sita continued to lament she cursed Manthara for having been the root cause of all her troubles and misery, and that of Dasharatha's family.

In the meantime, the good natured Suparswa, an upright and wise minister in Ravana's court, advised Ravana against slaying Sita. "Is it righteous for a younger brother of Kubera to kill a woman? Show your ire upon Rama alone, by challenging him to a fight. Do not malign yourself further by destroying Sita."

Ravana heeded Suparswa's judicious counsel and walked back to his palace.

Daring vanaras

The clash between the vanaras and demons continued ruthlessly. There was blood and gore everywhere and large parts of Lanka lay in ruins. The ogres went about hitting and killing everyone. Rama too was uncompromising. He destroyed the enemies' chariots, elephants, horses, demons and all. The rakshasa who were so overwhelmed by Rama's vicious assault upon them, cursed Soorpanakha for having incited and instigated Ravana to kidnap Sita and face the consequences of such an ignominious act. After all, was it not Soorpanakha who had egged Ravana on this path of destruction, to achieve her own end! The ogres recalled several instances that testified to Rama's supreme power and invincibility. Did Rama not single-handedly kill the monstrous Viradha and other mighty warriors and demons? Rama had dealt with so many of them, all alone. Were these deaths not enough to knock sense into Ravana and prompt him to restore Sita to Rama? If only our king had done this, Rama would have forgiven him. It would have ended the hostilities between them and we would have been spared this battle and bloodshed. If only Ravana had heeded Vibheeshana's and Kumbhakarna's wise counsel, we would not be facing misery and destruction today. The rakshasas wailed ruefully as they undoubtedly acknowledged Rama's supreme powers.

The ogres bemoaned the loss of their dear and near ones in a needless battle brought on by Ravana's impiety, arrogance and obstinacy. They recalled Shiva's promise to the gods when they sought his protection against the brutality of Ravana and his demons. "Did Shiva not tell the gods that a woman would bring about Ravana's downfall and thereby redeem them from the demons? Sita is that woman because of whom we will be wiped out! We have nowhere to go, nobody to turn to. Vibheeshana was indeed wise to join hands with Rama," the demons spoke amongst themselves and felt sorry for the fate that had befallen them.

Ravana joins the war

Ravana heard these laments from every home in Lanka. He was unperturbed. He instructed his men to march to the battle arena and vanquish Rama. He vowed to avenge the death of his brothers and sons. The entire Universe trembled as Ravana thundered down the streets of Lanka on his chariot, crossed the city gates and rode towards Rama. As he exited from the northern gate to confront his foe, the sun went down the horizon and darkness enveloped the city. There were omens portending misfortune -- a meteor fell from the skies, and clouds rained blood; crows and vultures emitted piercing and eerie cries while dogs howled. But Ravana marched forward, headstrong, claiming that Rama would not live to see the rising sun.

The vanara forces scattered and ran in all directions, felled by Ravana's missiles. Sugreeva rallied around them, reminding them of their noble cause. He seized a mammoth tree and armed with it, wrought untold destruction upon Ravana's army. He rained rocks on them causing them to crush under the weight of these boulders. Virupaksha, the demon commander of extraordinary power, mounted an elephant and attacked Sugreeva. A fierce war followed. Virupaksha's mount fell with a thud. The demon alighted from it and lunged upon Sugreeva. They fought like true warriors, falling down now and bouncing back in an instant. In a swift movement, Sugreeva struck Virupaksha on his temple bone, and killed him instantaneously. One by one, the stalwarts in Ravana's army fell in battle, defeated by Sugreeva and his forces. Angada killed Mahaparswa, one of the last among Ravana's most brilliant commanders.

With the fall of Mahaparswa, Ravana fought with redoubled vigour. Arrows and missiles covered the sky as Rama and Ravana confronted each other with their forces. Lakshmana fumed with fury as Ravana sent flurries of darts at Rama. He severed the head of Ravana's charioteer and smashed to bits, the demon king's bow. Vibheeshana struck down with his mace, the horses reined to Ravana's chariot. A beleaguered Ravana, who was now without his charioteer, leaped out of his vehicle. His face turned crimson and his eyes were blood shot with ire. He flung a sharp and pointed lance, poisoned at its tip, at Vibheeshana. But fortunately for Vibheeshana, Lakshmana intercepted it and split it into shards. The son of Dasharatha then ran towards Vibheeshana to protect him from the volley of arrows that Ravana hurled upon him. Ravana became furious and yelled at Lakshmana: "You chit of a mortal! I will kill you this very instant with my javelin which is infallible." The potent javelin was especially designed by the demon Maya for Ravana. The king of Lanka aimed it at Lakshmana's chest. The speed and force with which Ravana threw the weapon, it not only pierced Lakshmana's chest, but went through his body and into the earth and the Ikshvaku prince fell to the ground.

Rama's eyes welled up with tears as he saw Lakshmana fall to the ground, unconscious and bathed in blood. As he embraced his beloved brother, Rama asked Hanuman, Sugreeva and the rest of the vanara forces to stand guard over him while he himself fought Ravana. The combat between them gathered momentum and an assortment of weapons were employed. Ravana fled in fear when Rama closed in upon him.

Rama then turned his attention to Lakshmana who was lying motionless in a pool of blood, struggling to keep himself alive. Once again Rama was overcome by sorrow and wept bitterly. "Of what use would victory against Ravana be if I am to lose my beloved Lakshmana? Perhaps, with difficulty one may find a spouse as pious and chaste as Sita, but where would I find a brother such as Lakshmana! Without doubt I too shall give up my life if my dear brother were to depart from this world. What will I tell his mother Sumitra who dotes on him? How will I console her? O Lakshmana, warrior of exceptional skills, why do you lie so motionless, without even blinking an eyelid? Look at me, talk to me, dear brother! Open your eyes, wake up!"

Susena, a prime commander of the vanara force comforted Rama by telling him that Lakshmana was far from dead. He convinced Rama that his brother was alive, by pointing to the various vital bodily signs he observed in him. Once Rama regained his composure, Susena asked Hanuman to make haste and procure the life-saving herbs from the Mahodaya Mountains. Without delay, Hanuman swiftly proceeded to Mahodaya Mountain and returned in good time with huge chunks of the mountain containing the herbs. Lakshmana was restored to life and healed.

Rama embraced his sibling and held him close to his bosom, happy to see him spring back to life. Lakshmana immediately reminded Rama of his pledge to annihilate Ravana. He gently chided his older brother for displaying despondency and giving way to despair. "It is out of character for a prince of your stature and calibre to show such weakness in the face of slight adversity. It is high time you killed Ravana and rescued Mother Sita," Lakshmana urged Rama.

Lakshmana's spirited talk inspired Rama to resume his battle against Ravana.

Indra sends his chariot to Rama

Once again there was a relentless shower of armaments on the combat zone. Heaven and earth were lit up in flames and the earth was drenched in blood. The gods and demigods who witnessed the violence below from their celestial abodes expressed concern at the ill-matched combat. They found it unfair that while Rama stood on the ground, he faced Ravana who fought from his chariot.

Indra immediately summoned his charioteer Matali. "Take my chariot and serve Rama as charioteer in the war against the demon king of Lanka", he ordered. Indra also sent with Matali, his own bow, arrows, armour and spike for Rama to wield against Ravana and gain victory him.

As Matali descended from the heavenly world to the battleground, he stood before Rama and conveyed Indra's message to him and handed over the special arms to him. The goliaths, well matched in all respects, were now poised for an epoch-making battle. To the beating of war drums and blaring of trumpets, Rama and Ravana confronted each other in violent combat. Ravana shot thousands of arrows at Rama, pierced Matali with several shafts, struck the horses and tore apart Indra's chariot with a single arrow, bringing down its ensign. The seers, sages and divine beings agonized at Rama's plight. He was so overpowered by the continuous and aggressive assault upon him by Ravana, that he could barely fit the arrows to his bow! The gods kept cheering Rama, goading him to return triumphant in the encounter. Ravana maintained the momentum of his blitz on Rama. He pulled out one of his unassailable and most potent darts that was capable of annihilating all enemies at one stroke. Ravana's army was delighted to see their king raise the weapon against Rama. Ravana addressed Rama with great scorn and arrogance, "This most powerful dart will see you and your brother reach Yama's abode this very instant!"

Ravana gave a revolting laugh as he shot the dart at Rama. The weapon came hurtling forward with great velocity, making a deafening sound in its wake. Rama strung his bow with several arrows to intercept the deadly shaft, but to no avail. When Rama saw that his weapons were consumed by the gigantic spear sent by Ravana, he decided to use Indra's celebrated javelin which Matali had handed over to him. As the lance darted from the hands of Rama, a brilliant molten of lightning lit up the skies. Within moments, it split Ravana's fearful pike into myriad fragments and rendered it impotent. Rama then sent a barrage of arrows at Ravana which pierced him all over his body. Ravana was exhausted and felt stinging pain on his sides where the spears and pikes had struck him. He bellowed savagely in pain, anger and fear. He continued to fling all kinds of projectiles at Rama, who remained unflinching when struck by these missiles.

Rama addressed Ravana in a voice that was laced with sarcasm. "Yes, you are indeed a hero as you consider yourself to be, having carried away another's wife. You are undoubtedly a champion who whisked away a woman who was alone, helpless and unguarded. You should be ashamed of this heinous act, for having transgressed all moral codes and ethics. Today you shall aptly bear the fruits of all your gallant deeds."

Rama continued his onslaught of missiles at Ravana with reinforced vehemence. The monkeys were buoyed by Rama's spirits and they felled Ravana with rocks and crags. The Lankan king who was shelled by a torrent of weapons and huge objects from all sides, became dazed and confused. He was unable to think clearly and use the appropriate weapons on his enemy. Ravana's charioteer who perceived the king's befuddled state of mind, secretly led him away from the arena. Ravana became enraged at his charioteer's furtive action. He rebuked him with harsh words: "Why have you brought this ignominy upon me? Why did you, in such a surreptitious manner whisk me away from the battleground? Upon whose orders did you do this? Do you think I am a coward to run away from the attack of a mere mortal? Or is it that you have sold yourself to my enemy because you think I have become powerless and inefficient to defend myself?"

Ravana's charioteer patiently heard out the king's outburst. He then responded to Ravana's verbal volley by telling him that it was sheer affection for the king that made him withdraw from the field. "Oh king, you were extremely fatigued from the fight and were in no position to overcome your adversary. Your horses too were completely exhausted. There were ill omens that did not auger well for you to continue the combat. And above all else, is it not my responsibility as your charioteer, to assess the circumstances prevailing and then make a move in your best interests?"

Aditya Hridayam

Ravana was satisfied with his charioteer's explanation. He returned to confront Rama. Meanwhile Rama too was exhausted from the gruesome encounter with the demon king. As he stood surveying the situation and pondered over his next move, sage Agasthya appeared on the scene. He advised Rama to recite the supremely powerful and immortal 'Adithya Hridayam,' an ode to the Sun god. "This prayer propitiates Lord Brahma who is present in the orb of the Sun. Victory will certainly be yours my child, if you chant these verses. Prayer to the Sun God who is an embodiment of all gods, will enable you to conquer all your enemies," Agasthya explained to Rama.

Rama, heeded the words of the sage and prayed to the Sun god with due reverence and was all set with renewed vigor for a fresh conflict with the demon. As Ravana's grand and mighty chariot flew out of the gates of Lanka towards Rama, the scion of Ikshvaku cautioned Matali.

He asked him to be on guard and negotiate the chariot in a manner that would allow Rama to attack his opponent from a vantage point. Rama added, "My apologies to you Matali, for making these suggestions. I am aware of your high caliber and capability, and hence do not need to tell you what to do. Yet, I counsel you for I am extremely excited and agitated about vanquishing Ravana."

Matali was pleased to hear Rama's words. He deftly rode the chariot towards Ravana who hailed a torrent of arrows at Rama. Though Rama's anger was provoked by this barrage of weapons, he acted with patience and intelligence. He pulled out Indra's bow and arrows of extraordinary impulse and speed, and directed them at Ravana. The celestial beings gathered together in the skies to witness the fight, and waited and prayed for Ravana's defeat. Ravana's camp observed several foreboding signs while the vanara army saw propitious omens. As the combat headed to its climactic stage, Rama returned blow for blow and tore apart the ensign and flag of Ravana's chariot. A veritable second sky was created by the fearsome collision of weapons that illuminated the space between earth and heaven. As Ravana's spears stung Matali, Rama turned livid with rage. He sent a stream of darts against the demon. The duel between the goliaths continued unceasingly through day and night.

Ravana vanquished

Rama shot a serpentine arrow at Ravana, chopping off his head, only to find another take its place! As Rama severed Ravana's newly grown head, another sprung up in its place! This went on endlessly and left Rama ruffled. He wondered at the efficacy of his weapons which had, on earlier occasions, effectively destroyed so many ogres.

At this juncture, Matali reminded Rama to use the Brahmastra to vanquish Ravana. He said, "The hour of Ravana's doom as prophesized by the gods has arrived. It is time, O noble Rama, for you to use this most powerful weapon upon him."

Rama immediately pulled out the Brahmastra that was gifted to him by sage Agasthya. He aimed it at Ravana. The weapon emitted a fiery flame as it sped with lightning speed towards the king of Lanka. It pierced his chest and shattered it. Ravana's bow slipped from his hand. He gave a terrifying shriek and with a final cry of despair, fell down, dead. Ravana was vanquished.

All the Devas, gods and sages rejoiced at Rama's victory and showered flowers upon him. There was great jubilation among the vanaras.

Ravana's death lamented

While the vanara force felt intoxicated with joy, a pall of gloom enveloped Lanka as the ogres wailed for their fallen emperor. There were heart-wrenching cries in the city as its people mourned their illustrious king, who had brought destruction upon himself. Vibheeshana burst into tears on seeing his brother lie cold upon the bare earth, soaked in blood. "O beloved brother, you who were so learned, have met such an end! It pains me greatly to see you sprawled lifeless, rid of all glory and splendour! Why, dear brother, did you not heed my words, as I begged, beseeched and even admonished you, to give up the path of dishonor that you were treading upon?"

As Vibheeshana grieved for the departed soul, Rama consoled him saying, "Ravana lies defeated, not because he lacked valour or courage. He has reaped the consequences of his sins and has met his end for the good of the world.

He fought like a true warrior and therefore should not be mourned. We have accomplished our objective. It is only right that you perform his last rites as ordained by the scriptures."

Ravana's numerous consorts burst into loud wails, beating their chests and rolling on the ground. Mandodari, his queen agonized over his death. Even in grief she reasoned, "It is hard to believe that you, who remained undefeated by all gods including Indra, have met your end, at the hands of a mere mortal! I am convinced that it is Lord Vishnu himself in human form, helped by a pantheon of gods in monkey and bear forms, who has put you to eternal sleep. Did you not realize this fact when your brother Khara was killed single-handedly by Rama? How is it that you did not perceive it to be the handiwork of Vishnu when a mere monkey came to Lanka looking for Sita and left it, devastated?"

Mandodari was visibly shattered by her husband's death. She continued to lament, recollecting instances from the recent past. "You invited death by abducting Sita and casting evil designs on her. Did you not realize that her piety and chastity are an embodiment of fire that would consume you? Are some of your consorts not more beautiful than Sita! You were so smitten by her that you chose to remain stubborn even though Vibheeshana, Kumbhakarna, your grandfather and I pleaded with you on several occasions not to indulge in this act of adharma!"

None could stop Mandodari's outpourings as she continued, "I was proud of the three exceptional men in my life; you my husband, Maya my father, and Indrajit my son. All you glorious stalwarts, have now left me alone and gone to your graves. The curse of every woman who has been widowed because of you has brought about my widowhood." Mandodari fell upon her husband's inert body, weeping uncontrollably.

Rama then ordered Vibheeshana to perform Ravana's obsequies. Vibheeshana expressed his reluctance to complete the last rites to one who had strayed from the path of dharma. "Though I love him dearly as my brother, I have no respect for him. He tread the path of evil, aspired to make another's wife his own and needlessly brought harm upon several thousands of good souls. How can I perform his funeral rites?" Vibheeshana addressed Rama in all humility.

"Death ends all feelings of hatred and acrimony," Rama told Vibheeshana. "Your brother was brave and valiant and was never known to have been defeated in any battle. I have emerged victor and you have made contributions to this. It is only right that I show you my gratitude by guiding you to do what is right and befitting. In death, he is as much mine as he is yours. Our task has been accomplished and the onus rests on you to conduct the ceremonial rites for your brother's final journey. The world will sing your glory for upholding the tenets of dharma."

Vibheeshana's coronation

Vibheeshana performed Ravana's rites as advised by Rama. Matali ascended to his abode in the heavens after Rama expressed his profuse gratitude to him and to his master, Indra and bid him farewell. Rama then embraced Sugreeva for the tireless and unfailing assistance he had rendered along with his vanara force. The son of Dasharatha then called upon Lakshmana to make preparations for Vibheeshana's installation to the throne of Lanka. With due pomp and pageantry, Vibheeshana assumed kingship of Lanka.

At Rama's instance, Hanuman sought Vibheeshana's permission to proceed to Ashoka Vana to convey to Sita the happy news of Rama's triumph over Ravana. Tears flowed down Sita's face when she heard of Rama's victory. She looked at Hanuman in stunned silence, unable to express her joy. When she regained her composure she thanked the son of Vayu and praised him for the huge role he played in Rama's success against Ravana. Hanuman, with folded palms and head bowed, sought Sita's permission to kill all the female demons surrounding her. After all, had they not terrorized her and caused her immense misery!

Sita who was full of compassion, gently admonished Hanuman for wanting revenge. She said, "No. Noble son of Vayu, it does not befit you to kill them. They had only discharged their duty as ordered by their king. Now that he is dead, they will not harm me. Moreover, are you not aware of the age-old adage that was in reality spoken by a bear to a tiger? It runs thus, a man of superior virtues does not retaliate in a sinful manner, towards one who commits offence. It is not for the virtuous, to return evil for evil. The good and righteous, embellish themselves with right conduct even in the face of adversity and wickedness."

Sita rose still further in Hanuman's esteem when he heard her loving words. He took leave of her saying that she would soon see her beloved Rama.

Sita faces the fire ordeal

At Rama's behest, Vibheeshana met Sita at Ashoka Vana and informed her that she would soon be in the presence of Rama. He asked her to prepare herself appropriately for the occasion. In the meantime, Vibheeshana readied a majestic palanquin to carry Sita from Ashoka Vana.

As he announced Sita's arrival, Rama was overcome by an avalanche of mixed emotions. He was joyous and despondent in equal measure upon seeing his dear Sita who had lived for so long in the abode of a demon.

The monkeys and demons watched in fascination as Sita alighted from the palanquin and turned towards her beloved.

As she walked towards him, head bent low, Rama's heart swelled with love for this adorable lady who had been separated from him and had undergone untold suffering. Yet, when he spoke, his words were bereft of all emotion, and in fact, had a steely edge to them. "I have avenged your abduction and have rescued you from Ravana's evil intents. But you have lived in another man's dwelling for so long. How can I take back such a woman?"

Sita felt her heart pierced by a thousand arrows when she heard Rama's harsh words, uttered in the presence of all those assembled. Head still bent down, Sita addressed Rama in angry tones: "How is it that you speak to me in a manner that a common man would adopt towards an ordinary woman? Do you doubt my fidelity towards you? Is it that I willed myself to be carried away by the demon? Do you not believe that I became a victim of fate? Do you not believe that my mind and heart which alone are under my control, forever utter your name and have craved only for you? By speaking to me in this manner, you not only insult and pain me, but cast aspersions on my very character!"

Sita turned to Lakshmana and asked him to kindle a fire so that she could enter it to prove her chastity. Rama remained silent. The fire was prepared. Sita first circumambulated her husbad Rama who had disowned her and then approached the blazing fire.

She joined her palms in salutation to Agni and all the gods and addressed them in turn.

"My heart never parts from Rama. Even if Rama does not know this truth, surely Oh Agni, the witness of the world, you know it."

"In act, thought and speech, I've always been faithful to Rama. Even if Rama does not know this truth, surely Oh Agni, the witness of the world, you know it."

"Oh Surya, Oh Chandra, Oh Vayu, Oh devas of four directions, Oh devas of the day-time and the twilights and the night, and Oh Mother Earth, you are all witnesses to what I am, though Rama has turned blind to my virtues"

"Oh Agni the very embodiment of purity, I seek refuge in you."

As she went around the fire, the sages, gods, and the gandharvas gathered to witness Sita who was as pure as the sacrificial fire, seek refuge in that very element.

The assembly of gods, demi-gods, celestial beings, demons, people and vanaras, waited with bated breath to witness the truth. Sita, the epitome of virtue and righteousness, remained a picture of divine charm as she entered the blazing fire. For a moment, Rama was forgotten and all eyes remained fixed on Sita. She glowed with purity and serenity as she sought to become one with fire.

The congregation was unable to witness Sita's ordeal. They closed their eyes tight until they heard the divine voice of Agni. Now all eyes turned towards Agni who appeared in all his splendour with Sita alongside him. "Oh Rama, behold your Sita, who is as pure as ever. Sin cannot even touch this blessed lady who remains untainted of mind and body. I hereby order you to accept Sita with every honour due her!" Rama, his eyes brimming with tears rejoiced on hearing the fire god's words, even as Agni led Sita to him. The assembled crowd shouted in joy, "Hail Mother Sita, Glory be to her!"

Rama, who had appeared to be as hard as diamond a short while ago, now appeared to be as soft as a flower. His eyes welled with tears of joy. In a voice trembling with emotion, Rama spoke to Sita as he held her close to him. "Did I not know of your pure heart and mind, Sita? I knew in my heart, you are ever pure; but I wanted the whole world to know it. Now, no one can ever point a finger at my beloved, merely because she resided in the abode of Ravana! Come dear, your ordeals are over. Let us return to Ayodhya and join our loved ones."

There was much joy and merriment as Sita was reunited with Rama. But amidst all this rejoicing, Rama did not forget his vanara friends. He beseeched Indra to bring all the vanaras killed or maimed in battle, back to life and good health. Indra who acquiesced Rama's request, restored the vanquished monkeys and bears to life.

Rama's coronation

Rama had accomplished his task of annihilating Ravana. He duly oversaw Vibheeshana installed as king of Lanka. He now prepared to leave for Ayodhya as he had successfully completed his fourteen-year-term in exile. Rama politely declined Vibheeshana's invitation to prolong his stay in Lanka and partake of his hospitality. "I do not wish to delay my departure to Ayodhya because I am restless to see Bharata. I can barely wait to meet my dear brother," Rama responded.

The prince of Ayodhya thanked Vibheeshana profusely for his kindness and for being a most gracious host. However, since Rama wanted to reach Ayodha in quick time, he accepted Vibheeshan's offer of travelling to his kingdom by the Pushpaka Vimana, known for its incredible speed. Vibheeshana, Hanuman, Sugreeva and the entire vanara force expressed their ardent desire to accompany the princes to Ayodhya to behold the spectacular sight of Rama being crowned king. Rama who was overjoyed at this, gladly agreed to their request.

Together with Sita and Lakshmana, Rama ascended the Pushpaka Vimana, followed by the rest of their entourage. As the aerial car sped towards its destination, Rama pointed out to Sita the various spots where they had searched for her and how at each place he and Lakshmana had faced and destroyed ogres. En route, they made a brief halt at sage Bharadwaja's ashram to enquire after his welfare and that of the citizens of Ayodhya.

As they approached Ayodhya Rama asked Hanuman to convey the news of his imminent arrival to his cherished friend Guha. He also wanted Hanuman to proceed to his capital to learn of the welfare of its people, to know if they were happy under Bharata's stewardship. Rama asked Hanuman to apprise Bharata of all the events that had happened after Bharata's departure from Chitrakoota. Rama also asked Hanuman to observe Bharata's attitude, gestures, responses, reactions and facial expressions as he narrated Rama's trials and tribulations while in exile.

Rama confessed to Hanuman, "It is easy to become addicted to fame and fortune. Who would not want to covet such a kingdom as Kosala, which is endowed with abundant wealth? It is possible that having ruled the empire for so many years, Bharata now aspires to be its sovereign. If that is true, I would only be too delighted to see him as king of Kosala. It is important for me to know

Bharata's mind, Hanuman. Make haste and report to me, my brother's state of mind and that of my people."

Hanuman first met Guha and informed him of Rama's return. He left Guha dancing and crying in joy upon hearing such good tidings. Within a stone's throw from Ayodhya, Hanuman beheld Bharata, an emaciated figure, steeped in misery at having been parted from his beloved Rama. Hanuman observed that he lived like an ascetic, with matted locks, dressed in bark garments with skin of a black antelope tied around his waist. It was apparent that Bharata survived on fruits and roots alone and practiced austerities that only great seers undertook. When Hanuman approached him and told him that Rama was only a few miles away from him and Ayodhya, tears welled in his eyes and Bharata fainted, overwhelmed with joy. As soon as he recovered from the swoon and gained composure, Hanuman related Rama's story to him. Bharata heard him with deep anguish and shed copious tears as Hanuman recounted Rama's suffering and Sita's plight at Ravana's hands. When Hanuman concluded his narration, Bharata embraced him and promised to bestow upon him all kinds of wealth for bringing him the only news that he ever wanted to hear – of beloved Rama's return to Ayodhya.

The city of Ayodhya drowned in the nectar of joy at Rama's homecoming. A spirit of cheer and carnival atmosphere prevailed. Joyous shouts of "Here comes Rama. Here comes the glorious son of Dasharatha! Hail Rama our king," reached deafening proportions as the Pushpaka Vimana touched down at Ayodhya. Streets of the city were choked with people who came out to see their dearest prince. Bharata prostrated before his brother who gently picked him up and held him in a close hug. Tears flowed in a deluge when the brothers united. Bharata embraced Sugreeva and proclaimed him to be their fifth brother. "It is our good fortune that through the gesture of goodwill, you extended your hand in friendship to Rama. And is not a good friend, as good as a brother!"

Rama who had been most anxious to see Bharata, was relieved and happy to meet him. He then rushed to meet his mother Kausalya. She had become pale and weak from sorrow, having lost her husband and being separated from her son and daughter-in-law. Rama touched her feet and sought her blessing. He then paid his respects to Sumitra, and Kaikeyi, the queen mother who had brought him fame and had enabled the gods to be delivered from the misery wrought on them by Ravana and his demon race.

Ayodhya returned to a state of calm after the initial euphoria subsided. Bharata who had eagerly awaited Rama's return, addressed Rama most reverentially, and in all humility: "Beloved brother, it is now time for you to take charge of our kingdom which rightfully belongs to you."

The queen mothers, sages and scholars, and the council of ministers agreed with Bharata. Rama was crowned king in a grand celebration befitting royals, and Bharata was installed prince regent.

In the history of ancient India, Rama Rajya was a golden period where its people enjoyed peace and prosperity because it was ruled by an emperor known for his sense of justice and compassion. Nothing was more important to him than the welfare of his people who held him close to their heart. Dharma reigned supreme in the vast land, without a trace of greed, lust and avarice. The kingdom of Kosala witnessed no theft, no murders and no harassment of its womenfolk. It was a land where no father performed the funeral rites of a son, and no young woman was made a widow. Ayodhya and Kosala enjoyed Divine Bliss under Rama, who was ably assisted by his brothers, for thousands of years.